개정신판

TOURISM Hotel English Conversation

관광호텔영어회화

하종명 지음

Ha Jong Myong

Service isn't everything, it's the only thing.

– Van Nostrand Reinhold –

머리말

어느 무더운 여름 날 오후 우연히 교회를 짓고 있는 공사 현장을 지나가게 되었습니다. 그때 3명의 노동자가 일하는 모습을 보고 그들에게 똑같이 "이렇게 무더운 날씨에 무엇 때문에 쉬지 않고 일을 하십니까?" 하고 질문하였습니다. 그때 첫 번째 노동자는 "못죽어서 일을 하고 있습니다"라고 대답을 하였고, 두 번째 노동자는 "돈을 벌기 위해 일합니다"라고 대답을 하였으며, 세 번째 노동자는 "나는 신의 얼굴을 새기는 기분으로 일을 하고 있습니다"라고 대답을 하였습니다. 첫 번째의 경우는 일을 하면 그 일이 재미도 없고 능률도 오르지 못했을 것입니다. 두 번째의 경우는 첫 번째 대답을 한 노동자보다는 조금 더 재미있게 일을 하고 있었을 것입니다. 세 번째 대답한 분은 일이 참 재미있다고 생각하면서 일을 했을 것이고, 아마 능률도 있었을 것입니다. 호텔영어도 신의 얼굴을 새기는 기분으로 일을 하는 것과 같이 즐거운 마음으로 공부를 하게 되면 재미도 있고 실력도 향상될 것입니다.

호텔 종사원들은 호텔에서 업무를 수행하면서 영어를 사용하는 빈도가 상당히 높습니다. 그런데 영어를 유창하게 구사할 수 없어 업무 그 자체를 원활히 수행할 수 없는 경우를 많이 보았습니다. 이럴 때마다 호텔 종사원들이 업무를 수행할 때 어려움이 없는 책을 펴내야 되겠구나 하고 늘 생각해 왔습니다. 이러한 생각이 바탕이 되어 이 책을 쓰게 되었습니다.

이 책은 대학의 교재용으로 썼습니다. 나아가 호텔 종사원들의 업무 능력 향상과 호텔 영어를 동시에 익힐 수 있도록 구성하였습니다.

이 책의 Part One은 Room Division, Part Two는 Housekeeping Service, Part Three는 Food and Beverage Department, Part Four는 Handling Problem으로 구성되었고, Role Play와 토론 중심으로 쓰여졌습니다.

이 책이 출판되기까지 많은 도움을 주신 반주은 선생, 항상 말없이 적극적으로 지원하는 아내 이향숙, 아들 희찬, 태우에게도 고마움을 전한다. 또한 내외의 어려운 여건 속에서도 출판을 허락해 주신 백산출판사 진욱상 사장님과 편집실 여러분께 감사드립니다.

2013년 6월

저자 씀

Part 1 Room Division / 7

Part 2 Housekeeping Service / 111

Part 3 Food and Beverage Department / 153

Part 4 Handling Problems / 249

PART 1

Room Division

Lesson 1 Room Reservation

- Introduction
- Dialogue One
- Dialogue Two
- Dialogue Three
- Dialogue Four
- Dialogue Five
- Dialogue Six
- Dialogue Seven

Introduction

First Appearances

First appearances form lasting impressions, and it is simply good sense in hotel work to make sure that the guest gets a positive impression from the moment he walks into the lobby.

When a room clerk welcomes an arriving guest with courtesy, cordiality, and quiet confidence, he sets the tone for the guest's entire stay. Because this first encounter is so important in making a lasting impression, let's examine some traits that lead to a good first appearance.

A Sincere Friendly Smile

The sincere friendly smile is and has been a tradition of the hotel business for years. It can indicate that you are trying to be pleasant and courteous. However, it must be emphasized that the smile must be friendly; if it is wooden or a fixed expression that is turned on and off like an electric light, it may do more harm than good. An alert but unsmiling expression is probably more effective than the smile that means nothing.

Why are manners and appearance important for Service-man?

Dialogue One

(*C*: *Clerk* *G*: *Guest* *O*: *Operator*)

(Taking a reservation by phone)

O: Good morning, The JM Hotel, Miss Kang speaking. Can I help you?

G: I'd like to make a reservation. Would you put me through to the reservation desk?

O: Yes, I'll put you through to the reservation desk. Hold the line, please.

C: This is the reservation Office, Miss Kim speaking. May I help you, sir?

G: I am in Jinju City. I am going to Seoul and I need a room at your hotel from June 8th to 10th. Do you have rooms available?

C: We have a nice room available, sir. What type of room do you want?

G: A twin room, please. What's the rate of a twin room?

C: Twin rooms are 320 dollars per day. We have a room commanding a good view of the city.

G: OK. I'll take it.

C: May I have your name and phone number, please?

G: My name is Alan Douglas and my phone number is 751-8277.

C: Thank you for the reservation, Mr. Douglas. We will be waiting for you.

Key Points

* put ~ through to : ~에게 전화를 연결시키다.
* I'll put you through to the reservation desk.
  손님을 예약실로 연결시키겠습니다.
* We have a room commanding a good view of the city.
  도시 방향의 전망이 좋은 룸이 있습니다.

Dialogue Two

(***C*** : *Clerk* ***G*** : *Guest*)

(Asking the room rate)

C : Hello, reservation desk, Miss Kim speaking. May I help you?

G : Yes, I'm Smith. I'd like to make a reservation for a double room.

C : What date will you be arriving and how many nights do you plan to stay, Mr. Smith?

G : On June 9, for two nights.

C : Let me check, Mr. Matt. Just a moment, please.

G : Okay.

C : We have a room commanding a fine view for those dates, Mr. Smith. Have you stayed with us before?

G : No, I haven't, but I have a discount card.

C : Great. And what time do you expect to arrive on the 9th, Mr. Smith?

G : Let's see. I'll be there at 6 p.m. What's my room rate?

C : Our discounted rate is 320 dollars for a night, Mr. Smith. 10% tax and 10% service charge will be added. Is that okay?

G : Yes. I'll take it.

C : All right, Mr. Smith. I'd like to confirm your reservation.
That's a double room from June 9th to 11th. Your reservation number is JM75182. We look forward to serving you on June 9th.

G : Thank you.

C : You're welcome. Bye.

Key Points 

* What date will you be arriving and how many nights do you plan to stay?
  며칠날 도착하여 얼마나 체류하실 것입니까?
* What's my room rate? 객실요금은 얼마입니까?

Dialogue Three

(*C*: *Clerk* *G*: *Guest*)

(Procedure for paying the rate)

C: Good afternoon, reservation clerk, Miss Lee. Can I help you?

G: Yes. My name is Ron Bellugi. I want to make a reservation for two nights.

C: For what dates, Mr. Bellugi?

G: I expect to be there around 10 o'clock in the evening on July 13th.

C: Hold the line, please. I'll check for you, Mr. Bellugi. We have a double room available for those dates. I suggest you make a guaranteed reservation with a credit card. This ensures that your room will be held after our 7 p.m. cancellation policy. you can arrive any time that evening and your room will be waiting for you. Please call us before 7 p.m. if you have any changes to your plans, Mr. Bellugi. Would you like to make a guaranteed reservation?

G: I will make it. Do you take Visa card?

C: Yes, we do. May I have your card number and expiration date?

G: Yes, 5588-3356-8847-8912. The Expiration date is 07/15.

C: Your Visa card number is 5588-3356-8847-8912 and the expiration date is July, 2015. Do you have any questions?

G: No, that's it.

C: OK, Mr. Bellugi. Thank you for your reservation. Then we look forward to seeing you in our hotel.

G: Thanks.

C: My pleasure, Mr. Bellugi. Have a good day.

Key Points 

* I suggest you make a guaranteed reservation with a credit card. 카드로 예약보장을 하시는 것이 좋을 것입니다.
* May I have your card number and expiration date? 손님의 카드번호와 만기 날짜를 말씀하여 주시겠습니까?

Dialogue Four

(***C***: *Clerk* ***G***: *Guest*)

(Reservations are fully booked)

C: This is the reservation desk. How may I help you?

G: I'd like to make a reservation in your hotel.

C: For what dates?

G: I'll be arriving on July 20th and staying for three days. I would like to have a double room. Is there one available?

C: Let me check. Just a moment, please. I'm very sorry, sir.
We don't have any double rooms left for those dates.

G: How about a twin room?

C: Unfortunately, we have a full house for those dates. We have only a suite available.

G: How much is it?

C: 600 dollars for a night.

G: That's too expensive for me. I'd like to have something less expensive. Could you recommend another hotel?

C: Yes. I can. I know a hotel with reasonable prices around here, sir. Shall I call for you, sir?

G: I'd really appreciate it. I'll call back later.

C: Yes, sir. I'll call that hotel for you. Good bye.

Key Points

* For what dates? 며칠날 오시겠습니까?
* We have a full house for those dates. 그 기간에 모든 객실이 만실입니다.
* I know a hotel with reasonable prices near here.
  여기 근처에 가격이 적절한 호텔을 알고 있습니다.

Dialogue Five

(***C***: *Clerk* ***G***: *Guest*)

(Confirmation of the reservation)

C: This is the reservation desk. May I help you?

G: Yes. I'd like to confirm my reservation.

C: Do you have a reservation number, sir?

G: No. I don't.

C: Who's the reservation for, sir?

G: I'm Frank Lewis.

C: For what day, Mr. Lewis?

G: I'll be there tomorrow.

C: Hold the line, please. I'll check the list. I'm sorry to have kept you waiting, Mr. Lewis. Your room is confirmed for that day. Your reservation number is JM8277, Mr. Lewis. If you have any questions, your reservation number will help you easily. Is there anything else I can do for you, sir?

G: No, that's all.

C: We look forward to seeing you then.

G: Oh, thank you. See you then. Good-bye.

Key Points 

* Do you have a reservation number?
예약번호가 있습니까?

* Who's the reservation for?
어느 분 이름으로 예약이 되어있습니까?

Dialogue Six

(***C***: *Clerk* ***G***: *Guest*)

(Making the reservation again due to a mistake)

C: Good afternoon. Reservation desk, Miss Lee speaking. May I help you?

G: Yes, please. My name is John Brown. I've got a reservation for a double room for two nights.

C: What are the dates of your visit, Mr. Brown?

G: June 10th.

C: I'll check on that. One moment, please. Sorry, Mr. Brown. We don't have any reservation listed for you. When did you make your reservation?

G: I made it two weeks ago by telephone.

C : Sorry, Mr. Brown. I've looked it over carefully. I still can't find your name.

G : Something must be wrong.

C : Excuse me, we have twin rooms for those dates. Can you have a twin room, Mr. Brown?

G : What's the room rate?

C : 310 dollars per night, Mr. Brown.

G : Okay. I'll take it. I'd like some place where it is quiet.

C : Yes, I'll do that. We'll arrange it on June 10th just for two nights. That's a twin room facing the beach on the second floor. I think that'll be most suitable for you. We shall be waiting for you. Thanks for calling.

G : Thank you. It's very kind of you.

Key Points

* I've got a reservation for a double room for two nights.
  2일 간 더블 룸을 예약했었다.
* Something must be wrong.
  무엇인가 잘못되었습니다.
* I think that'll be most suitable for you.
  그 룸이 당신에게 가장 적절하다고 생각한다.

Dialogue Seven

(***C*** : *Clerk* ***G*** : *Guest*)

(Cancelling the reservation)

C : This is the reservation office, Miss Kim speaking. May I help you?

G : Yes, I'd reserved a room at your hotel from March 9th to 11th. But my schedule has changed. I want to cancel my reservation.

C : Okay. Do you know your reservation number, sir?

G : No. I don't.

C : Who made the reservation, sir?

G : My name is Jim Stone.

C : I'm sorry, I didn't get your name. Will you spell it for me, please?

G : Jim Stone, J-I-M S-T-O-N-E.

C : Thank you, Mr. Stone. I'll check on your reservation and have it cancelled, Mr. Stone.

G : I'm sorry about it this time.

C : It's quite all right. I hope we can serve you in the future, Mr. Stone.

G : I hope so, too.

C : Thanks for your early notice, Mr. Stone. Have a nice day.

G : Thanks. Bye.

Key Points 

* I want to cancel my reservation. 예약을 취소하고 싶다.
* Who made the reservation? 누구의 이름으로 예약을 했습니까?
* I'll check on your reservation and have it cancelled.
  예약을 확인하고 취소하겠습니다.

■ Language Choices 1

1. I'd like to make a reservation for a double room.
2. I want to make a reservation for a single room.
3. I'd like to reserve a room for two nights.
4. I'd like to book a room, please.

■ Language Choices 2

1. I'd like to get a room.
2. Do you have any rooms tonight?
3. Can I put up at your hotel tonight?
4. Can I stay at your hotel tonight?
5. Can I get a room at your hotel for tomorrow night?
6. Is there a room available tonight?

■ Language Choices 3

1. How long will you stay here, ma'am?
2. How long are you planning to stay, sir?
3. How long are you going to stay here, ma'am?
4. For how many nights do you wish to stay, sir?

■ Language Choices 4

1. What are the rates for the rooms?
2. What's the rate of a single room?
3. What's the rate of the room per night?
4. What's the daily rate?
5. May I know the room rate?
6. What's the tariff?
7. Can you tell me what is the room rate?
8. I'd like to know the rate.

■ Language Choices 5

1. We're fully booked.
2. All double rooms are fully booked for June 20th.
3. There are no vacancies those dates.
4. We have full occupancy tonight.

■ Language Choices 6

1. What type of room do you want, sir?
2. What kind of room would you like, ma'am?
3. What kind of room would you like to have, sir?
4. Do you want a double room or twin room, sir?
5. Would you like a single room, ma'am?
6. We could give you only a single, ma'am.

Practice

Step 1. Please fill the gaps in this conversation with the words below. Use each word or expression once.

> guaranteed reservation / room rate / how many nights / listed / a full house / cancelled /Who's / any changes

1. Would you like to make a ____________________?
2. Please call us before 7 p.m if you have ________________ to your plans.
3. We have ____________________ for those dates.
4. What's my ____________________?
5. We don't have any reservation ____________________ for you.
6. ____________________ the reservation for, sir?
7. What date will you be arriving and ________________ do you plan to stay?
8. I'll check on your reservation and have it ____________________.

Step 2. Discuss with your partner or group.

1. Make a list of information you need from the guest to make a booking.
2. What information will the guest need from you about your hotel?
3. Why is it important to check or confirm all information?
4. Listening to English can sometimes be difficult. Think of 3 ways you can politely ask the guest to repeat what he is saying.
   EX) "I'm sorry, sir. Could you say that again?"

Reading

Read the following story and answer the questions with five minutes.

■ Room Reservation

The booking system of the service department is very important, as most hotel customers make a reservation in advance. Reservation clerks play a vital role in customer service, because they often give the first impression of the hotel to their customers. In addition, reservation clerks should always be prepared to respond to any inquiries regarding hotel services and facilities confidently to guests, and also to strangers.

Reservations can be made through phone, internet, correspondence, fax, or by verbal request. When customers request a reservation, the reservation clerk must record their personal details including name, contact number, room rates, room types, the arrival/departure date, and a payment method. In addition, the reservation clerk must bear in mind to confirm the availability status to customers.

Questions for Discussion

1. Why are reservation clerks the first contact for customers?
2. Why should reservation clerks be familiar with all internal hotel information?
3. What methods are used by customers when making a room reservation?
4. What personal details of customers must be recorded when making a reservation?

Role Play of Reservation Clerk

1. Do a role play reserving a hotel room.
2. Do a role play in the situation in which a guest has to make a reservation again due to a mistake by the reservation clerk.
3. Do a role play cancelling the reservation.

Lesson 2 Doorman Service

- Dialogue One
- Dialogue Two
- Dialogue Three
- Dialogue Four
- Dialogue Five

Dialogue One

(***D*** : *Doorman* ***G*** : *Guest*)

(Offering help with baggage)

D : Good afternoon, ma'am. Welcome to the Grand JM Hotel.
May I help you with your baggage, ma'am?

G : No, thanks. It's not so heavy. I'll take it by myself. By the way, where can I register?

D : You can register at the front desk over there, ma'am.

G : Where is the front desk?

D : Go through the lobby and mind your hands in the revolving door, please.
It turns very quickly.

G : Thank you for your kindness.

D : You're welcome. Have a pleasant day.

Key Points

* May I help you with your baggage?
  손님의 수화물을 도와드릴까요?
* I'll take it by myself.
  제가 들어도 됩니다.

Dialogue Two

(***D***: *Doorman* ***G***: *Guest*)

(Carrying luggage)

D: Good afternoon, Mrs. Brown. Thank for visiting our hotel again.

G: Thank you for recognizing me.

D: I know you stayed at our hotel two weeks ago.

G: Even though I stayed here then, I'm surprised that you recognize me.

D: Ah, is that so? That's my jobs, too. May I help you with your luggage, Mrs. Brown?

G: Thanks. I have some luggage. Don't forget to bring my luggage from the trunk.

D: Don't worry, ma'am. I'll bring all of your luggage.

G: Please take care of my luggage very carefully. There are some fragile things in it.

D: Certainly, sir. ma'am I'll leave them here and our bellman will take care of it.

G: Thanks. I'll be at the front desk.

Key Points 

* Don't forget to bring my luggage from the trunk.
  트렁크에 있는 수화물을 가져오는 것을 잊지 마세요.
* I'll bring all of your luggage.
  모든 수화물을 가져올게요.

Dialogue Three

(***D*** : *Doorman* ***G*** : *Guest*)

(Car parking)

D : Good afternoon, Mr. Lewis. Nice to meet you again. Thank you for visiting our hotel. How long will you stay, Mr. Stone?

G : Two nights. Can you park my car in the parking lot?

D : Sure, Mr. Lewis. We'll take care of everything. Enjoy your stay, Mr. Lewis.

G : That's very kind of you. Thanks for your help.

D : My pleasure.

Key Points

* Can you park my car in the parking lot?
  주차장에 차를 주차하여 주실 수 있습니까?
* We'll take care of everything. 모든 것을 잘 보살필 것입니다.

Dialogue Four

(***D*** : *Doorman* ***G*** : *Guest*)

(Calling a car)

D : How are you this afternoon, sir?

G : Fine. Could you get my car?

D : Yes, sir. What's the number?

G : It's 6781.

D: Wait a moment, please. I'll get it right away, sir. 6781 comes to the front door. Your car will be here in few minutes.

(After a while)

Here comes your car, sir

G: I really appreciate it.

D: Have a great day.

Key Points 

* Could you get my car?
 차 좀 가져다주시겠습니까?
* I'll get it right away.
 곧 가져오겠습니다.

Dialogue Five

(***D***: *Doorman* ***G***: *Guest*)

(Calling a taxi)

D: Good morning, sir. Are you leaving today?

G: Yes. I need a taxi. Can you call a taxi for me?

D: Certainly, sir. Where is your destination?

G: I'd like to go to Gimhae International Airport.

D: Wait a moment, please. I'll call it right away, sir. A taxi will be here after a while.

G: Thanks. I'm going to take the flight at Gimhae International airport at three o'clock. How long does it to get there?

D: It takes about one hour, sir. You have enough time, if you take a taxi now.

G: What's the taxi fare to Kimhae?

D: Less than 15,000 won, sir.

G: Okay.

D: Did you enjoy your stay here, sir?

G: Yes, it was very good.

D: It's very hot outside. Please wait in the lobby, sir. I'll tell you when a taxi arrives.

G: Thanks. I'll wait in the lobby.

(After a while)

D: Here came the taxi, sir. I'll put your suitcase and luggage in the trunk.

G: Thanks for your help.

D: You're welcome. Have a good day. Please come again, sir.

Key Points

* Can you call a taxi for me?
  택시를 불러 줄 수 있습니까?
* I'll put your suitcase and luggages in the trunk.
  트렁크에 여행용 가방과 수화물을 실어 드리겠습니다.

■ Language Choices 1

1. May I help you with your baggage?
2. May I take your baggage for you?
3. How many bags do you have?
4. Do you have any baggage in the trunk?
5. Don't forget to bring my luggage from the trunk.

■ Language Choices 2

1. Can you park my car in the parking lot?
2. You can't park in front of the main door, sir.

■ Language Choices 3

1. What's the license number of your car?
2. I'll call it right away, sir.

■ Language Choices 4

1. Can you take the hotel shuttle bus?
2. Shall I call a taxi for you?
3. I'd like to take a taxi.

Practice

Step 1. Use the words or phrases in the box to fill in the spaces below.

enough time / bring / register / the lobby / take / right away / take care / What's

1. Please ____________ of my luggage very carefully.
2. You can ____________ at the front desk over there.
3. You have ____________, if you take a taxi now.
4. I'll ____________ it by myself.
5. Please wait in ____________, sir. I'll tell you when a taxi arrives.
6. I'll get It ____________.
7. I'll ____________ all of your luggage.
8. ____________ the taxi fare to Kimhae?

Step 2. Discuss with your partner of group.

1. Some people say the doorman has the most important job in the hotel. Why?
2. Why are first impressions the most important impressions?

Reading

Read the following story and answer the questions with five minutes.

■ Doorman Service

It is important to note that doormen generally give the first impression of the hotel when greeting a customer. Therefore they should make efforts to act proudly and with a positive and respectful attitude, to properly represent the hotel's image. The major roles of doormen include opening and closing car doors to assist customers who are entering or exiting the hotel, and controlling the traffic at the hotel entrance.

They also play an important role in greeting customers upon entrance as well as giving a farewell upon exit. Furthermore, they have the responsibility of working with the bellman to deliver customers' baggage without any mistakes, and also to provide transportation services at the customers' convenience.

Questions for Discussion

1. Why do you think doormen are crucial in influencing the hotel's overall image?
2. Let's talk about the duties of doormen.
3. What attitudes should doormen display while working?

Role Play of Doorman

1. Do some role plays in guest reception procedures.
2. Do some role plays in seeing the guest off.

Lesson 3 Bellman Service

Dialogue One

(***B***: *Bellman* ***G***: *Guest*)

(Ushering a guest from the bell desk to the elevator)

B: Good afternoon, sir. May I help you?

G: Yes, please. All of these suitcases and bags are mine.

B: Okay. I'll carry them to the front over there. After checking in, I'll show you to your room, sir.

G: Oh, Thank you.

(After a while)

B: There is the elevator right over there. We'll take your baggage to your room, sir.

G: I see.

B: May I have your room key, please?

G: Here you are.

B: Thanks. Your room is on the 8th floor. We'll go up in the elevator. This way, please.

(After a while)

Please take the elevator. After you, sir.

G: Thanks.

B: This is the 8th floor. Here we are. After you, sir.

(Get out of the elevator)

Your room is 802 to you left. Here is your room, sir.

Please get in first.

G: This room looks comfortable. How do I call room service?

B: Please dial 6, sir.

G: Thank you. Excuse me, I need to write some letters. Where are they?

B: In the desk drawer, sir. Is there anything else, sir?

G: That's all. I appreciate it.

Key Points 

* I'll show you to your room. 손님을 객실로 안내할 것입니다.
* We'll take your baggage to your room. 수화물을 객실로 운반할 것입니다.
* We'll go up in the elevator. 엘리베이터로 올라 갈 것입니다.

Dialogue Two

(***B***: *Bellman* ***G***: *Guest* ***C***: *Front clerk*)

(Asking the bellman to show the guest to his room from the front clerk)

C: Please take Mrs. Brown's bags to room 913.

B: Good afternoon, Mrs. Brown. Do you have only these two bags?

G: No, I have two more suitcases over there. Please bring them, too.

B: Yes, Mr. Brown.

C: Her room is 913. Here's her key.

B: Please come this way. We'll take the elevator to your floor. Please watch your step when you get on the elevator, Mrs. Brown.
(The elevator door open)
Come this way, please. Here is your room.

G: It's a very nice room. Oh, it's a wonderful view of the river.

B: I'm happy that you like it, ma'am. Let me put your bags and suitcases on the luggage stand. And the temperature control is on the wall. Please call us if you need any help.

G: How do I call the bell desk?

B: Please dial 2.

G: Thank you very much for your kindness.

B: It's my pleasure. Have a nice stay with us.

Key Points 

* Let me put your bags and suitcases on the luggage stand.
  수화물대에 여행용 가방들을 두겠습니다.
* The temperature control is on the wall. 온도조절 장치는 벽에 있습니다.
* Please call us if you need any help. 도움이 필요하시면 전화 주십시오.

Dialogue Three

(***B***: *Bellman* ***G***: *Guest*)

(Showing the guest around the hotel room)

B: Good afternoon, let me show you to your room, ma'am. Have you ever been to our hotel before?

G: No, this is my first time.

B: This way, please. We're on the 8th floor, ma'am.
Room 810 is on your right, ma'am.
(Unlock the door and switch on light)
This is your room. After you, ma'am. Please get in. I'll put your baggage here, ma'am.

G: That's good.

B: If you leave the key card in the holder, the light will work, ma'am. Here's the light switch for the bathroom. The night table has all the switches for the room lights. Here is some stationery. The closet is here. And your mini-bar is in the cabinet over there.
A price list is inside the drawer. You'll be charged for what you use when you check out. There are also a room service menu and a brochure listing all the services of the hotel on the table. There are several channels on cable TV.

This information shows how to use the cable TV.

G: Oh, very good. By the way, how do I call room service?

B: Please dial 6, ma'am. Room service operates 24 hours a day.

You can make use of it at any time, ma'am. As for the telephone, please dial 1 for the front desk, 2 for the bell desk, dial 3 for laundry or 5 for housekeeping. Please call the front desk if you need anything.

G: Oh, what time does the beauty shop open?

B: Until 9 p.m, ma'am. Have a pleasant stay with us, ma'am.

G: I really appreciate it. This is for you.

B: I'm sorry, ma'am.

We have a no tipping system in our hotel.

Key Points 

* Let me show you to your room. 방을 안내해 드리겠습니다.
* Room service operates 24 hours a day. You can make use of it any time.
  룸서비스는 24시간 운영됩니다. 언제든지 룸서비스를 이용할 수 있습니다.
* You'll be charged for what you use when you check out.
  퇴숙하실 때 사용한 것에 대해서는 요금이 부과됩니다.

Dialogue Four

(***B***: *Bellman* ***G***: *Guest*)

(When the wrong baggage has been carried to the room)

B: (Knocking at the door) Bell Service. I brought your bags, sir.

G: Just a moment. (Opening the door) Come on in.

B: I'm really sorry for the delay, sir. I have three pieces here. Is this the correct number of bags, sir?

G: Oh! These bags are mine, but that isn't mine.

B: Are you sure, sir?

G: Yes. I'm positive. It's not mine.

B: Can you describe your bag, sir?

G: My bag looks like this one, but it has a different brand. It's a similar size. I have a name tag on it. There must be some mistake.

B: I'm really sorry, sir. That was probably our mistake, sir.
I'll go down and check with the bell captain again, sir.
And then I'll be back with the correct bag right away.

G: All right. I'll wait for you.
(After a while)

B: Is this your correct bag, sir?

G: Yes, it's mine.

B: I'm really sorry for the inconvenience, sir.

G: That's okay.

B: Enjoy your stay, sir.

Key Points

* Is this the correct number of bags?
  가방의 개수가 맞습니까?
* I'll be back with the correct bag right away.
  곧 손님의 가방을 가지고 오겠습니다.
* I'm really sorry for the inconvenience.
  불편하게 해서 정말 미안합니다.

Dialogue Five

(***B*** : *Bellman* ***G*** : *Guest*)

(Carrying the guest's suitcases when checking out)

G : Hello, is this bell desk?

B : Yes, this is Mr. Kim at the bell desk. May I help you?

G : Yes, please. I'm going to check out right now. Can you send a bellman up to my room 813 to take my suitcases?

B : Room 813? I'll send our bellman up right away, sir. Could you wait in your room for a while, please?

G : Sure. (After a while)

B : Good morning, sir. I'll bring down your suitcases. How many suitcases do you have?

G : Just three.

B : I'll take your suitcases down to the lobby near the front cashier's desk, sir. Could you bring the other small bags?

G : Of course. I'll bring them. Thanks.

B : You're welcome.

(After a while)

G : (At the bell desk) Where are my suitcases?

B : Here you are.

G : I'll come here again when I need a hotel.

B : Have a great day, sir.

Key Points

* I'll send our bellman up right away. 곧 벨맨을 보내드리겠습니다.
* How many suitcases do you have? 가방이 몇 개입니까?

Dialogue Six

(***B*** : *Bellman* ***G*** : *Guest*)

(Asking to keep baggage at the cloak room)

B : Good morning, sir. May I help you?

G : Yes, please. I'm going to go to Jeju and come back tomorrow. But I'm worried about my baggage. So I'd like to leave them here while I'm in Jeju. Can you look after my baggage?

B : All right, sir. We can keep your baggage in the cloak room, sir. Please fill out this form. Is there anything valuable or breakable in your baggage?

G : No, there isn't.

(After a while)

B : This is your baggage tag, sir. You are supposed to show it to me when you want your bags again, please.

G : Thanks a lot. Please take good care of them.

B : Certainly, sir. What time do you want them back, sir?

G : I'll be back by twelve o'clock.

B : That's fine. See you then, sir.

Key Points

* We can keep your baggage at the cloak room.
  수화물 보관소에 수화물을 보관할 수 있습니다.
* Is there anything valuable or breakable in your baggage?
  수화물 안에 귀중품이나 깨지기 쉬운 것이 있습니까?
* You are supposed to show it to me when you want them again.
  수화물을 다시 원할 때 저에게 그것을 보여주십시오.

■ Language Choices 1

1. I'll show you to the front desk.
2. I'll show you to your room.

■ Language Choices 2

1. This way, please.
2. Please come with me.

■ Language Choices 3

1. I'll bring your baggage to your room.
2. I'd like to deliver these things to a room.
3. I'll bring a luggage cart.
4. I'll carry your bags to your room right away.

■ Language Choices 4

1. You'll be charged for what you use from the mini-bar.
2. You'll be charged for what you drink.

■ Language Choices 5

1. We'll send the bellman up right away.
2. Our bellman will be there in a moment.

Practice

Step 1. Use the words or phrases in the box to fill in the spaces below.

take / temperature / go up / call / charged / put / sorry / valuable or breakable

1. Let me ___________ your bags and suitcases on the luggage stand.
2. Please ___________ us if you need any help.
3. You'll be ___________ for what you use when you check out.
4. We'll ___________ in the elevator.
5. The ___________ control is on the wall.
6. I'm really ___________ for the inconvenience.
7. We'll ___________ your baggage to your room.
8. Is there anything ___________ in your baggage?

Step 2. Discuss with your partner or group.

1. Why is the bellman's service important to the customer?
2. How can the bellman offer the best service to the customer?

Reading

Read the following story and answer the questions with five minutes.

■ Bellman Service

In general, bellmen greet their guests as they enter the lobby, and inform or sometimes guide them to the hotel's service department, restaurants, and other facilities. Bellmen carry out numerous tasks that include: delivering customers' luggage to their rooms after check-in, guiding them to their room individually, and showing them how to use the telephone and other facilities in the room.

The work responsibilities of bellmen are as follows: firstly, they must always be respectful to their customers; secondly, they must smile when they serve; thirdly, they must practice courteous and polite wording; fourthly, they must maintain tidy and clean grooming; and lastly, they must perform their tasks efficiently and with sincerity until complete.

Questions For Discussion

1. What duties do bellmen perform?
2. What should bellman be aware of and pay more attention to while performing their tasks?
3. What are the customer service duties of bellmen?

Role Play of Bellman

1. Do role plays in doing check-in, ushering in guests the front, carrying baggage, accompanying guests to the elevator and to the hotel room.
2. Do role plays in carrying guest's luggages promptly to the rooms, explaining how to use the rooms and facilities in the hotel.
3. Do role plays in offering prompt and accurate service to guests checking out.

Lesson 4 Front Clerk Service

- Dialogue One
- Dialogue Two
- Dialogue Three
- Dialogue Four
- Dialogue Five
- Dialogue Six
- Dialogue Seven

Dialogue One

(*C*: *Front Clerk* *G*: *Guest*)

(Check-in for reserved guests)

C: Welcome to the HYATT hotel. May I help you, ma'am?

G: Yes, I'd like to check in.

C: Excuse me, did you make a reservation, ma'am?

G: Yes, I made a reservation for three nights.

C: May I have your name, ma'am?

G: My name is Jane Jackson.

C: Wait a moment, please. Mrs. Jackson, I'll check the list. We have a double room ready for you on the 9th floor for three nights.

G: Very good.

C: Please fill out this registration card, Mrs. Jackson. You must fill out this card; name, nationality, passport number and so on, please. May I see your passport for a moment, please?

G: Certainly, here it is.

C: Thank you. Sign here, please.

G: Okay.

C: Thank you, Mrs. Jackson. Here is your card key. Your room number is 918 on the 9th floor. And the bellman will show you to your room. I hope you have a pleasant stay, Mrs. Jackson.

G: Thank you very much.

Key Points

* Please fill out this registration card. 이 등록 카드를 작성하여 주십시오.
* The bellman will show you to your room.
  벨맨이 룸에 안내해 드릴 것입니다.

Dialogue Two

(***C***: *Front Clerk* ***G***: *Guest*)

(Check-in for a guest who has not made a reservation)

C: Good evening, sir. Do you need any help?

G: Yes, please. Do you have any rooms available for tonight?

C: Excuse me. Did you make a reservation, sir?

G: No, I didn't. I'd like a double room if you have any vacant rooms.

C: Just a minute, please. Let me check that for you, sir.

(After a while)

Sorry, sir. Our double rooms are already full. We only have twin rooms.

G: How much do they cost?

C: 380 dollars per night plus 10% tax and 10% service charge, sir.

G: Okay. I'll take one for tonight. I'd like a quiet room.

C: Yes, you will find this room perfectly quiet, sir.

G: Does the rate include breakfast?

C: No, it doesn't. Do you have any other special requests that our hotel can provide, such as a non-smoking room?

G: Yes, non-smoking room, please. And I'd like to have a room near the ground floor, if possible.

(After a while)

C: I'll get you a non smoking room near the ground floor. Please fill in this registration card.

(After a while)

Here's your room key, sir. How about the 3rd floor?

G: Very good. Thank you.

C: You're welcome. Your room is 319. Our check-out time is 12 o'clock.

G: I'll keep it in mind. Thank you so much.

C: Have an enjoyable stay, sir.

Key Points 

* Let me check that for you. 확인해 보겠습니다.
* Our double rooms are already full. 더블 룸이 이미 만실입니다.
* Our check-out time is 12 o'clock. 퇴숙 시간은 12시입니다.

Dialogue Three

(***C***: *Front Clerk* ***G***: *Guest*)

(Giving information on another hotel when no rooms are available)

C: Hello. May I help you?

G: Yes, we'd like to get a room.

C: Did you make a reservation, sir?

G: No, we didn't. I'd like a quiet twin room if you have any vacant room.

C: When would you like to stay here, sir?

G: Tonight.

C: I'll check the list. Would you mind waiting for a moment?

G: Sure.

C: Sorry, sir. We're fully booked tonight. Shall I find another hotel for you?

G: Great, thank you.

C: We'll do our best. May I have your name, please?

G: Jim Stone and Thomas Anderson.

C: I'll call around for you.

G: Thank you.

C : You're lucky, sir. I'd like to recommend you to the JM hotel.

G : Where is it ?

C : Located in Itaewon Dong not far from here, sir. Here's a map with the address and please show this to the taxi driver. He'll take you there. The telephone number is 751-8277.

G : Thank you very much for your help.

C : You're welcome.

Key Points 

* Would you mind waiting for a moment? 잠시만 기다려 주시겠습니까?
* We're fully booked tonight. 오늘 이미 예약이 완료되었습니다.
* Shall I find another hotel for you? 제가 다른 호텔을 찾아볼까요?

Dialogue Four

(***C*** : *Front Clerk* ***G*** : *Guest*)

(Asking to have a room with a fine view)

G : Hi, I made a reservation here on-line.

C : Welcome to the JM Hotel.
May I have your name, sir?

G : My name is Jonathan Thomas from the USA.

C : Just a moment, please. We have a reservation for you and your wife, Mr. Thomas. Will you stay here for two nights from October 6th?

G : Yes, that's right. I want a room with a king-size bed. Do you have a room available like that?

C: Yes, Mr. Thomas. We have a room on the 9th floor facing the ocean. I want to recommend room 915, if you like.

G: That'll be fine.

C: This is your registration card. May I have the spelling of your first and last name, passport and phone number?

G: J-o-n-a-t-h-a-n T-h-o-m-a-s. My passport number is AG 38616781 and my phone number is 751-8277.

C: Can you just check through the details before signing here?

G: Certainly.

C: Here's your card key, Mr. Thomas. The bellman will show you up to your room right away. Wait a minutes, please. I'll have a bellman help you with your suitcases, Mr. Thomas.
Enjoy your stay here, Mr. Thomas.

G: Thank you for your kindness.

Key Points 

* Do you have a room available like that?
그런 방을 이용할 수 있습니까?
* We have a room on the 9th floor facing the ocean.
9층에 바다 방향의 객실을 드리겠습니다.
* I want to recommend room 915, if you like.
손님께서 좋아하신다면, 915호를 추천하고 싶습니다.

Dialogue Five

(***C***: *Front Clerk* ***T***: *Tour Escort*)

(Check-in for a group of guests)

C: Can I help you, sir?

T: Yes, my name is Jonathan Thomas. I'm the escort for the JM tour group from LA. We've just arrived.

C: Welcome to the JM hotel, Mr. Thomas. We've been waiting for your group.

T: Are our rooms ready for check-in?

C: Of course, they are. We've reserved nineteen twin rooms and one single room for thirty-nine people.

T: That's right. May I see the rooming list?

C: Here you are. Shall I set up a master account for your group?

T: Yes, please. Put the rooms and meals on it, but not other bills. Our baggage will be arriving soon. It should be forty pieces in total.

C: Forty. Okay.

T: We have them all labeled. Would you mind having your porter deliver them to each room according to the list?

C: Certainly, sir. Your baggage will be delivered by the bellman soon.

T: Thank a lot.

C: When will you check out tomorrow morning, sir?

T: It will be at 9:30 a.m.

C: That's good, sir. If you place your baggage in front of your room by 9:00 a.m. tomorrow morning, our bellman will pick them up.

T: Yes, we'll do that.

C: Shall we arrange a morning call at 7 a.m.?

T: Yes, please.

C: What time will you have your breakfast tomorrow morning, sir?

T: How about 7:30? Where can I change some money?

C: Our cashier will be happy to help you right over there.

T: Thanks.

C: We'll have your breakfast ready at the coffee shop on the first floor by 7:30 a.m. Anything else I can do for you?

T: No. I guess that's all.

C: I hope you have a good time with us here.

Key Points 

* We've been waiting for your group.
  우리는 손님의 단체를 기다리고 있었습니다.
* Your baggage will be delivered by the bellman soon.
  수화물은 곧 벨맨이 운반하여 드릴 것입니다.
* Our bellman will pick them up. 벨맨이 그것들을 가지려 갈 것입니다.

Dialogue Six

(***C***: *Front Clerk* ***G***: *Guest*)

(Asking to make out the bill prior to check-out)

C: How are you this afternoon?

G: fine.

C: Can I help you, sir?

G: Yes, please. We'll check out tomorrow morning.

C: May I have your name and room number, please?

G: My name is Jack Martin and the room number is 1208.

C: Just a moment, please.

What time do you expect to leave?

G: I expect to leave at around 11 o'clock.

C: I'll have the cashier make out your bill, sir.

G: Very good, sir. Shall we put our baggage outside the room?

C: Yes, sir. Please leave them there. And our bellman will take care of them. Please ask your guests to bring the other small bags themselves.

G: Of course. We'll do that. We'll be back at that time.

C: See you then, sir.

Key Points 

* What time do you expect to leave?
  몇 시에 떠날 예정입니까?
* I'll have the cashier make out your bill.
  회계원에게 영수증을 작성하도록 하겠습니다.
* Please leave them there. 그것들을 거기에 두십시오.

Dialogue Seven

(***C***: *Front Clerk* ***G***: *Guest*)

(Asking to deposit valuables)

C: Good morning, ma'am. May I help you?

G: Yes, please. I'd like to have this jewelry kept here. I have to go to Busan because I have a meeting. And I'll be back here tomorrow evening.

C: That's fine. We'll put your valuables in the safety deposit box, ma'am. Would you please fill out this form?

G : Yes.

(After a while)

Here you are.

C : Here's your key, ma'am.

G : Thank you for your kindness.

C : It's my pleasure.

Key Points

* I'd like to have this jewelry kept here.

  이 보석을 여기에 보관하고 싶습니다.

* We'll put your valuables in the safety deposit box.

  귀중품을 안전 보관함에 넣어 둘 것입니다.

■ Language Choices 1

1. Please fill out this registration card.
2. Please fill in this registration form.
3. Please register here.
4. Would you please fill in this registration card?

■ Language Choices 2

1. We've made your reservation.
2. Your reservation has been made.
3. We made a reservation.

■ Language Choices 3

1. I want to check in.
2. I'd like to check in.

■ Language Choices 4

1. The bellman will take you up to your room.
2. I'll have a bellman take your suitcase.
3. The bellman will carry your baggage to the room.
4. Your baggage will be delivered by the bellman.

Practice

Step 1. Use the words or phrases in the box to fill in the spaces below.

recommend / fill out / check / full / find/ make out /kept

1. Our double rooms are already ___________.
2. Shall I ___________ another hotel for you?
3. Let me ___________ on that for you.
4. Please ___________ this registration card.
5. I want to ___________ room 915, if you like.
6. I'll have the cashier ___________ your bill.
7. I'd like to have this jewelry ___________ here.

Step 2. Discuss these questions with a group of three or four students.

1. What does "A guest's problems are an employee's to solve" mean?
2. How can an employee solve a guest's complaints?

Reading

Read the following story and answer the questions with five minutes.

▪ Front Desk Clerk Service

Because front desk clerks are the first to greet customers upon their arrival, it is crucial that they offer good first impressions of the hotel. Front desk personnel must offer bright and courteous impressions to their guests and positively affect the image of the hotel. Also, they must always think from the customers' perspective and approach their tasks with a compassionate and understanding attitude.

Customers are the only people that recognize hotel employees' existence. They are the only people that can contribute to the growth and development of the staff and the hotel, and give them satisfaction from their jobs. Ellsworth M. Statler once said, "Life is service. The one who progresses is the one who gives his fellow men a little more, a little better service." Front desk clerks must keep this in mind as they carry out their services.

Questions For Discussion

1. Why do you think front desk personnel are important?
2. What is considered a desirable performance of front desk clerks?
3. Why do you think customers can provide job satisfaction and fulfillment for both employees and hotel management?
4. What is the meaning of the phrase, "Life is service"?

Role Play of Front Desk Clerk

1. Do a role play in reception and check-in procedures.
2. Do a role play in giving guest information on another hotel when no rooms are available in our hotel.
3. Do a role play in cooperating with a tour escort to offer group guests the best service.

Front Cashier Service

- Dialogue One
- Dialogue Two
- Dialogue Three
- Dialogue Four
- Dialogue Five
- Dialogue Six

Dialogue One

(***C***: *Front Cashier* ***G***: *Guest*)

(Asking to pay by credit card)

C: Good morning, ma'am. May I help you?

G: Well, I'd like to check out now. I was in room 726.
Can you make out my bill?

C: Just a moment, please. Did you use your mini-bar, Mrs. Wilson?

G: No, I didn't.

C: It comes to a total of 350 dollars, Mrs. Wilson. Here is your bill.

G: Can I pay with an American Express card?

C: Yes, Mrs. Wilson. Would you give me your passport, please?

G: Here you are.

C: Thanks. Would you please sign here on the bottom?

G: Yes, please.

C: Thank you. Here's your card and passport, Mrs. Wilson. I hope you enjoyed your stay with us, Mrs Wilson.

G: It was great. My stay in your hotel has been very pleasant.

C: Thank you for patronizing our hotel. We look forward to serving you again in the near future, Mrs. Wilson.

Key Points 

* It comes to a total of 350 dollars. 총합계가 350달러입니다.
* My stay in your hotel has been very pleasant. 호텔에서 즐겁게 보냈습니다.
* Thank you for patronizing our hotel.
  저희 호텔을 이용해 주셔서 감사합니다.

Dialogue Two

(***C*** : *Front Cashier* ***G*** : *Guest*)

(Paying an additional rate)

C : Good morning. May I help you, sir?

G : Yes, please. I'll be checking out at 3 p.m. I'd like to use it till three o'clock. What's the extra room charge?

C : The time for our hotel check out is 12:00 noon, sir. If you'd like to keep your room till three o'clock, you have to pay 30% as an extra charge. That's our hotel's rule, sir.

G : That's OK. How much will that be?

C : Your charge is 60 dollars, sir. May I have your room number?

G : 912. Do you accept traveler's check here?

C : Yes, we do. Just a moment, sir. Your bill totals to 320 dollars.

G : Here you are.

C : Would you please sign here, sir?

G : Okay.

C : Excuse me, may I have your room key?

G : Here it is. I have enjoyed my stay here.

C : Thank you very much. I hope you have a good trip.

Key Points

* The time for our hotel check out is 12:00 noon.
  퇴숙 시간은 12시입니다.
* You have to pay 30% as an extra charge.
  할증요금으로 30%를 지불하여야 합니다.
* That's our hotel's rule. 그것은 우리 호텔의 규정입니다.

Dialogue Three

(***C*** : *Front Cashier* ***G*** : *Guest*)

(Asking to correct a miscalculated bill)

G : Hi, I'm going to leave now. I'd like to pay my bill. Here is my room key.

C : May I have your name and the room number, sir?

G : Bill Jones, 1235.

C : Just a moment, please. Here's your bill, sir. Your bill comes to 350 dollars.

G : Just a minute. Perhaps there is a mistake. What's this charge for 20 dollars marked 'B'? Please explain me about it.

C : 'B' is a charge for the Main Bar. Did you get anything to drink at the Main Bar?

G : No. I haven't been to the Main Bar.

C : I'll check again, sir. Wait a minute, please.

G : Sure.

C : These are signed here, room 1234.

G : Oh! No. My room number is 1235.

C : I'm really sorry. I charged the bill to the wrong room by mistake. I'll correct this right away.

G : That's okay.

C : Thank you for checking it, sir.

Key Points 

* Your bill comes to 350 dollars.
350달러입니다.

* What's this charge for 20 dollars marked 'B'?
B로 표시된 이 20달러는 무엇을 의미합니까?

Dialogue Four

(***C*** : *Front Cashier* ***G*** : *Guest*)

(Asking to exchange foreign currency)

C : Good morning, sir. What can I do for you, sir?

G : Yes. Can I change money here?

C : Yes, you can. We're authorized, sir.

G : I'd like to change U.S dollars into Korean money.

C : How much do you want to change?

G : Two hundred dollars, please. What's the exchange rate today?

C : The exchange rate is 1,130 won for one dollar today, sir.

G : Okay. Here you are.

C : Please fill out this form. May I see your passport?

G : Sure. Here you go.

C : How will you be settling your bill, sir?

G : I want all ten thousand won notes.

C : It comes to 226,000 won, sir. Here are your notes. And here is your change, 6,000 won and your receipt, sir.

G : Thanks a lot.

C : Have a nice day, sir. Good-bye.

Key Points

* I'd like to change U.S dollars into Korean money.
  U.S 달러를 한국 원화로 바꾸고 싶습니다.
* What's the exchange rate today? 오늘의 환율은 얼마입니까?
* The exchange rate is 1,130 won for one dollar today.
  환율은 1달러에 1,130원입니다.

Dialogue Five

(***C***: *Front Cashier* ***T***: *Tour Guide*)

(Check-out for group guests)

T: Hello, I'm the tour guide of Hana. We'll leave in two hours. Would you be ready for our bill?

C: Certainly, sir. When will you come down here?

T: Let's see. How about 1:30 p.m?

C: Very good, sir. And then we'll make up the bill for your master account.

T: Okay. I need two copies of the bill, please.

C: Yes, we'll do so.

T: Well, shall we put our baggage outside the room?

C: Yes, sir. Our bellman will take care of them. Please have your guests bring the other small bags themselves, sir.

T: Of course. We'll do that.

(After a while)

Here are our keys. They are 25 keys.

C: Thank you, sir.

Your amount comes to 3,750 dollars. How do you want to make the payment?

T: I'll pay it by Visa card.

C: May I have your signature here, please?

T: Sure. Here you go.

C: I hope you enjoyed your stay, sir. Please come again.

T: Yes, we'll do that.

Key Points

* We'll make up the bill for your master account.
  손님의 계산서를 준비하겠습니다.
* How do you want to make the payment? 어떻게 지불할 것입니까?
* I'll pay it by Visa card. 비자카드로 그것을 지불할게요.

Dialogue Six

(*C*: *Front Clerk* *T*: *Tour Guide*)

(Asking to separate the bill)

C: Good morning, sir. I'm sorry to have kept you waiting so long. May I help you?

G: Yes, please. I have to check out now. Here's my key to room 725.

C: Thank you. Was everything satisfactory?

G: Yes, everything was so good.
Could you make out two separate bills for me? I'll pay for my laundry, drinks and all other charges. My company will pay for my room and meals.

C: Yes, sir. I'll draw up two bills for you, sir.

G: Thank you.

C: Thank you for waiting, sir. Your total amount comes to 400 dollars. How would you like to pay for this?

G: I'll pay all the bills in cash.

C: Thank you so much. Have a nice day.

Key Points

* Could you make out two separate bills for me?
계산서를 두 장으로 나누어 작성할 수 있습니까?

* My company will pay for my room and meals.
나의 회사는 객실과 식사요금만 지불합니다.

* I'll draw up two bills for you.
나는 손님을 위해 두 장의 영수증을 작성하겠습니다.

■ Language Choices 1

1. I want to settle my bill.
2. I'd like to pay my bill.
3. I'd like to pay my account.
4. Please have our bill ready.
5. Can you make out my bill?

■ Language Choices 2

1. May I have your room number?
2. Could you give me your room number?
3. What's your room number?
4. What room did you stay in?

■ Language Choices 3

1. Your bill comes to 200,000 won.
2. It comes to 250,000 won.
3. Your bill totals 210,000 won.
4. Your total amount is 250 dollars.
5. Your folio comes out at 220 dollars.
6. Your charge is 180 dollars.
7. That's 150 dollars in total.

■ Language Choices 4

1. How would you like to pay?
2. How will you pay your bill?
3. How do you want to make payment?
4. Will you pay in cash?
5. Will you pay by a credit card or with traveler's checks?

■ Language Choices 5

1. We look forward to seeing you again.
2. I hope we'll see you again.
3. Please come again.
4. We look forward to serving you soon.
5. We hope to welcome you again soon.
6. See you again.
7. We hope to see you again.

Practice

Step 1. Use the words or phrases in the box to fill in the spaces below.

make up / exchange rate / separate / extra charge / comes to / signature / use / pay / change / rule

1. Could you make out two ___________ bills for me?
2. How would you like to ___________ for this?
3. I'd like to ___________ U.S dollars into Korean money.
4. Your total amount ___________ 400 dollars.
5. May I have your ___________ here, please?
6. The ___________ is 1,130 won for one dollar today.
7. That's our hotel's ___________.
8. You have to pay 30% as an ___________.
9. Did you ___________ your mini-bar?
10. We'll ___________ the bill for your master account.

Reading

Read the following story and answer the questions with five minutes.

■ Front Desk Cashier Service

Front desk cashiers are responsible for payment and key collection/ distribution during customer check-ins and check-outs. Aside from accounting, front desk cashiers offer foreign exchange services as well as storage of personal valuables. Front desk cashiers should express their sincere gratitude to customers and ask for their feedback on the strengths, weaknesses and opportunities for the hotel before saying their final goodbyes.

The front cashier's tasks are as follows: they must post customers' bills into customer's personal account; they should confirm customer payments during check-outs; they should collaborate closely with the accounting department when demanding payment of a customer, either to their credit card company or the firm that the customer may represent.

Questions For Discussion

1. Why should front desk cashiers request customer feedback regarding the hotel's level of service and satisfaction?
2. What are the tasks of front desk cashiers other than receiving payment from customers?
3. What are the final procedures for front desk cashiers before they finish their shifts?

Role Play of Front Cashier

1. Do role plays of a guest and the front cashier when checking out.
2. Do role plays of a guest and the front cashier assuming that the guest wants an extension and that there has been a miscalculation in the bill.
3. Do role plays when the guest wants to exchange foreign currency.
4. Do role plays when group guests check out.

Lesson 6 Information Service

- Dialogue One
- Dialogue Two
- Dialogue Three
- Dialogue Four

Dialogue One

(***C*** : *Information clerk* ***G*** : *Guest*)

(Offering information on the hotel facilities, case Ⅰ)

C : Good afternoon. Can I help you, sir?

G : I want to have some Korean food. Could you recommend some restaurants for our dinner?

C : Yes, sir. I'd like to suggest your dinner at "Mukungwha", the Korean restaurant on the third floor.

G : That sounds great. We'd like to have various kinds of Korean food.

C : You'd better reserve a table, sir.

G : Yes, we think so. Is it expensive?

C : I think it's not as expensive as you might expect.

G : That's good. Could you make a reservation for us at 7 p.m.?

C : Sure, sir. May I have your name, please?

G : My name is Donald Hamilton.

C : We'll be glad to reserve a table for you.

G : Thanks a lot. It's very kind of you.

C : Don't mention it.

Key Points 

* Could you recommend some restaurants for our dinner?
  저녁 식사를 위해 레스토랑을 추천해 줄 수 있습니까?
* I'd like to suggest your dinner at "Mukungwha", the Korean restaurant on the third floor. 3층에 있는 한식당, 무궁화에서 저녁 식사를 하시는 것이 좋을 것으로 추천합니다.
* I think it's not as expensive as you might expect.
  너무 비싸지도 않을 것으로 생각합니다.

Dialogue Two

(***C*** : *Information clerk* ***G*** : *Guest*)

(Offering information on the hotel facilities, case Ⅱ)

C : Hello, what can I do for you, sir?

G : I'm looking for a barber shop in the hotel. Could you tell me where it is?

C : Sure, sir. We have a barber shop in the first basement. Go down to the 1st basement floor and turn right next to the souvenir shop, please. You can't miss it, sir.

G : Please reserve a seat for me.

C : Yes, sir. What time do you want, sir?

G : It would be better at four o'clock for me.

C : All right, sir.

Key Points

* Go down to the 1st basement floor and turn right next to the souvenir shop, please.
  지하 1층으로 내려가서 기념품가게 다음에서 오른쪽을 돌아가십시오.
* You can't miss it. 그곳을 반드시 찾을 수 있을 것입니다.

Dialogue Three

(***C*** : *Information clerk* ***G*** : *Guest*)

(Shopping recommendations)

G : Excuse me. I'd like to go shopping after dinner. Could you recommend some places for shopping?

C : Well, there are many good places for shopping, but I'd like to recommend Itaewon. We say Itaewon is a "shopper's heaven" for sports wear, shoes, leather and eel skin products.

G : Good. How can I get there?

C : How about taking a taxi?

G : How long does it take to get there?

C : It'll take 15 minutes from here by taxi, sir.

G : What's the taxi fare?

C : Maybe it'll be about 4,500 won, sir. This is the hotel's card. Please show it to the taxi driver.

G : Okay, let's take a taxi.
Thank you for your kind information.

C : You're welcome. Have a good time, sir.

Key Points

* There are many good places for shopping, but I'd like to recommend Itaewon.
쇼핑할 곳이 많이 있습니다만, 이태원을 추천하고 싶습니다.
* How long does it take to get there?
거기에 가는데 얼마나 걸립니까?
* It'll take 15 minutes from here by taxi.
택시로 15분 정도 걸립니다.

Dialogue Four

(***C*** : *Information clerk* ***G*** : *Guest*)

(Offering information on attractions)

G : Excuse me, I'd like to take a trip around Seoul. But I don't know where to go. Would you recommend some good places to visit in Seoul?

C : Yes, sir. I can recommend to you many palaces, the national museum, the Namsan mountain and many markets.

G : That sounds fantastic! Where are they?

C : It's not far from here.

G : How can I get there?

C : You can use a city tour bus leaving at our hotel or a rental car, but it would be convenient to use a city tour bus for you.

G : Could you reserve a seat for me right now?

C : Yes, sir. It starts at 9 a.m. and 10:30 a.m. The pick-up is in front of our hotel.

What time is more convenient for you, sir?

G : I'd like to leave at 10:30. Thanks for your kind help.

C : You're welcome, sir. Shall I give you a map of Seoul, sir?

G : Yes, please.

C : Here you are. Have a nice trip, sir.

Key Points 

* I can recommend to you many palaces.
  많은 궁전을 추천할 수 있습니다.
* It's not far from here. 여기서 멀리 떨어져 있지 않습니다.
* Shall I give you a map of Seoul? 서울 지도를 드릴까요?

■ Language Choices 1

1. Could you recommend some restaurants for our dinner?
2. Can you suggest some good places for our dinner?

■ Language Choices 2

1. I suggest a Korean restaurant.
2. I suggest you have your dinner at a French restaurant.
3. I'd like to recommend you have your dinner at the Korean restaurant.

■ Language Choices 3

1. Could you recommend some good places for shopping(sight seeing)?
2. Can you tell me something about shopping?
3. Where is the best place to go shopping in Seoul?

■ Language Choices 4

1. What's the best way to get there?
2. How can I get there?
3. Can you tell me how to get there?

Practice

Step 1. Use the words or phrases in the box to fill in the spaces below.

looking / reserve / The pick-up / recommend / convenient / give / expensive / show / get

1. I'm ___________ for a barber shop in the hotel.
2. Shall I ___________ you a map of Seoul?
3. Please ___________ it to the taxi driver.
4. I think it's not as ___________ as you might expect.
5. Please ___________ a seat for me.
6. ___________ is in front of our hotel.
7. It would be ___________ to use a city tour bus for you.
8. How long does it take to ___________ there?
9. Could you ___________ some restaurants for our dinner?

Step 2. Discuss with your partner or group.

1. What tourist attractions in Seoul would you recommend to your guests? Why?
2. Can you read a Seoul map in English? Next time you are in Seoul pick one up and bring it to class.
3. How do you get to the school restaurant from your classroom?

Reading

Read the following story and answer the questions with five minutes.

■ Information Service

The main role of the information service is to respond to inquiries from customers. Every information service must be equipped with in-depth knowledge about their job and their hotel to enable them to respond to all questions without fail. If a information clerk is uncertain about a question, they should show their customers reference materials and provide attitudes of attempting to collaborate with them to find the answer. This appeals to customers more positively.

The inquiries made by customers are generally limited, and typically concern the hotel, guide of the city or province, transportation, and location and features of shopping centers. Information clerks must always have this information ready. However, because this information is subject to frequent change, there is a need to update it regularly. To provide the customers with optimum satisfaction, information clerks must obtain accurate, relevant, and sufficient information.

Questions For Discussion

1. What should a concierge do when they have a difficult question to answer?
2. Let's talk about what inquiries customers can make to concierge desk?
3. How should concierges prepare to give customers appropriate and accurate information?

Role Play of Information Clerk

1. Do a role play in giving a guest information on restaurants and facilities.
2. Do a role play in giving information on shopping areas and tourism destinations.

Lesson 7 Operator Service

- Dialogue One
- Dialogue Two
- Dialogue Three
- Dialogue Four
- Dialogue Five

Dialogue One

(***O*** : *Operator* ***G*** : *Guest*)

(Asking for a morning call)

O : This is the operator. Can I help you?

G : Yes, please. This is Mr. Green in room 1105. I have to catch a plane at 10:00 a.m. I'm afraid I may fall into a deep sleep. Can you give me a morning call at 7:00 a.m. tomorrow morning?

O : Certainly, sir. We'll call you at exactly 7:00 a.m, Mr. Green.

G : Thank you. I'll rely on you.

O : Don't worry about that, please. Have a nice sleep, Mr. Green.

(The next morning at 7:00 a.m.)

O : Good morning. This is your morning call. It's 7:00.

G : Thanks a lot. I'll get up right away.

O : Have a good day, sir.

Key Points

* Can you give me a morning call at 7:00 a.m. tomorrow morning?
  내일 아침 7시에 모닝콜을 주시겠습니까?
* We'll call you at exactly 7:00 a.m.
  정확하게 오전 7시에 전화를 드리겠습니다.

Dialogue Two

(*O* : *Operator* *G* : *Guest*)

(Transferring a call to the guest)

O : Good afternoon, JM hotel operator. Can I help you?

G : Yes, I'd like to talk to Mr. Brown in room 1613.

O : May I ask who's calling, sir?

G : Mr. Jones.

O : Hold on, please.

(After a while)

I'm sorry, Mr. Jones. There's no one in room 1613. Would you like to leave a message, Mr. Jones?

G : OK. Please tell him to call me when he comes back. My phone number is 751-8277.

O : I'll do that for you, Mr. Jones. Do you need anything else?

G : No, thanks a lot. I believe that is all.

O : I'll give him the message as soon as he comes back, Mr. Jones. Have a nice day.

Key Points

* May I ask who's calling?
  전화하시는 분이 누구신지 여쭈어도 됩니까?
* Would you like to leave a message?
  메시지를 남기겠습니까?
* I'll give him the message as soon as he comes back.
  그가 돌아오시면 곧 그에게 메시지를 전하겠습니다.

Dialogue Three

(***O***: *Operator* ***G***: *Guest*)

(Asking to make a long distance call)

O: Operator speaking. May I help you?

G: I'd like to make a long distance call to Busan. How can I call?

O: You can dial directly. You have to dial 9 first, and then the number you want.

G: I see. Thanks a lot.

O: My pleasure.

Key Points 

* I'd like to make a long distance call to Busan.
  부산에 시외전화 하고 싶습니다.
* You have to dial 9 first, and then the number you want.
  처음에 9번을 돌리시고, 손님께서 원하시는 번호를 돌리시면 됩니다.

Dialogue Four

(***O***: *Operator* ***G***: *Guest*)

(Asking to make an overseas call)

O: Good evening. What can I help you with?

G: This is Mr. Brown in room 723. I'd like to make an overseas call to Sydney.

O: You can dial the number directly yourself in your room.

G: I did just now, but I had a bad connection with a lot of static.

O: OK. I'll try it for you, Mr. Brown. What number are you calling, Mr. Brown?

G: The area code is 6 and the number is 256-2456.

O: Thank you, Mr. Brown. Could you hang up the phone, Mr Brown? I'll ring you when your party is on the line.

G: Yes. Thank you.

Key Points 

* I did just now, but I had a bad connection with a lot of static.
  내가 지금 막 했지만, 소음으로 인하여 연결이 나빴습니다.
* Could you hang up the phone? 전화기를 놓아 주시겠습니까?
* I'll ring you when your party is on the line.
  상대방이 나올 때 제가 손님께 전화 드리겠습니다.

Dialogue Five

(***O***: *Operator* ***G1***: *Guest*, ***G2***: *Guest*)

(Asking to make a collect call)

G1: Hello, I'd like to make a collect call to New York.
The phone number is area code 312, then 751-8322.

O: All right. May I know who's speaking and the room number, ma'am?

G1: Mrs. Brown, room number 508.

O: Who would you like to speak to, ma'am?

G1: I'd like to speak to Mrs. Smith.

O: Mrs Brown. Hold on a second.

O: (After a while)
Hello, could I speak to Mrs. Smith?

G2: Speaking.

O: Will you accept a collect call from Mrs. Brown in Seoul?

G2: Yes, I'll pay the charge.

O: One moment, please. Here's your party now, Mrs. Brown. Go ahead, please.

G1: Thank you, operator.

Key Points

* May I know who's speaking and the room number?
전화하시는 분과 객실번호를 제가 알아도 됩니까?
* Who would you like to speak to? 누구와 대화를 하고 싶습니까?
* Will you accept a collect call from Mrs. Brown in Seoul?
서울에 있는 Mrs. Brown씨로부터 collect call을 받드시겠습니까?

■ Language Choices 1

1. Who's calling, please?
2. Who's speaking, please?
3. Who‘s this calling, please?

■ Language Choices 2

1. I'd like to place a long distance call to Seoul.
2. I want to make a long distance call to Busan.
3. I'd like to make a collect call to Sydney.
4. I'd like to make an overseas call to Japan.

■ Language Choices 3

1. Who do you want to speak to?
2. Who would you like to connect with?
3. To whom do you want to speak?

■ Language Choices 4

1. Sorry, there's no answer.
2. Sorry, nobody is answering.
3. Sorry, no one answers the phone.

■ Language Choices 5

1. Hold the line, please.
2. Hold on a moment, please.
3. Hold on a second, please.

■ Language Choices 6

1. You have a call.
2. You are wanted on the phone.
3. There's a phone call for you.
4. A phone call for you.

Practice

Step 1. Use the words or phrases in the box to fill in the spaces below.

make / no / dial / ring / fall into / exactly / message / directly / speaking / accept

1. There's ___________ one in the room 1613.
2. We'll call you at ___________ 7:00 a.m.
3. I'd like to ___________ an overseas call to Sydney.
4. May I know who's ___________ and the room number?
5. You have to ___________ 9 first, and then the number you want.
6. I'll ___________ you when your party is on the line.
7. I'm afraid I may ___________ a deep sleep.
8. I'll give him the ___________ as soon as he comes back.
9. You can dial the number ___________ yourself in your room.
10. Will you ___________ a collect call from Mrs. Brown in Seoul?

Step 2. Discuss with your partner or group.

1. What information do you need from your guest to make a call for them?
2. Should you check the phone number? Why?
3. What is a collect call?
4. What does "please hold the line" mean?

Reading

Read the following story and answer the questions with five minutes.

■ Operator Service

Telephone operators act as a bridge between hotel guests and those who try to call them from outside the hotel. The vocal timbre and intonation of operators can often determine whether or not a business call is successful. Although operators' smiles and other positive facial expressions cannot be viewed through the phone, the cheer and happiness in their voices can still help to deliver those same messages.

The tasks of telephone operators include: connecting customers on the phone, receiving phone calls and facsimiles, offering a morning call service, making long distance or international calls, reporting telephone bills or business logs, and responding to outside calls. Especially, the morning call service can be critical to hotel guests and should be timed precisely. Failure in doing so can easily affect the punctuality of the customers and cause business failures, from missing flights, trains, and other types of transportation, resulting in customer complaints and a bad reputation and image for the hotel.

Questions For Discussion

1. Why are telephone operators considered as vital and essential staff members?
2. How can telephone operators' smiles and laughter be transmitted to the customer?
3. Let's talk about the tasks of telephone operators.
4. What is the morning call service, and why must it not be taken lightly?

Role Play of Operator

1. Do a role play of making a morning call for the guest.
2. Do a role play asking for a long distance or overseas call.
3. Do a role play of asking to make an overseas collect call.

Lesson 8 Business Service

- Dialogue One
- Dialogue Two
- Dialogue Three
- Dialogue Four
- Dialogue Five

Dialogue One

(***C*** : *Clerk* ***G*** : *Guest*)

(Asking to mail a letter)

C : Good morning, ma'am? What can I do for you, ma'am?

G : Sure. I'd like to send this letter to my company in New York.
I have to rush.

C : Don't worry, ma'am. We'll take care of your mail.
I'll send it by DHL.

G : How much do I have to pay for it?

C : It's 13,000 won, ma'am. Shall I transfer it to your room account?

G : Great! How long will it take to get there?

C : It takes about a week. Could you tell me your name and room number?

G : Certainly. My name is Jane Jackson and the room number is 905.
Thank very much for your help.

C : You're most welcome. Have a nice day.

Key Points

* I'll send it by DHL.
DHL로 그것을 보내드리겠습니다.
* Shall I transfer it for your room account?
그것을 손님의 객실 계산서로 돌려드릴까요?

Dialogue Two

(***C***: *Clerk* ***G***: *Guest*)

(Asking to send mail by express post)

C: Good afternoon, sir. How can I help you?

G: I'd like to send this letter to L.A.

C: Do you want to send this letter express, sir?

G: Yes, please. I'm in a hurry. And this is a very important letter.

C: Would you put it on the scale there, sir?

G: Okay.

C: It costs ten dollars, sir.

G: Here you are.

C: Thank you. I'll be happy to send it for you.

Key Points 

* Do you want to send this letter express?
  급행으로 이 편지를 보내시길 원하십니까?
* Would you put it on the scale there?
  그것을 거기 저울 위에 올려주시겠습니까?

Dialogue Three

(*C* : *Clerk* *G* : *Guest*)

(Asking to make photocopies)

C : Good afternoon. What can I do to help, sir?

G : I'd like to copy these documents.

C : Certainly, sir. Please give them to me, sir.

G : Here you are. I'd like to make five copies of this document and three of these documents. When will they be ready?

C : They will be ready within five minutes, sir. Shall I bring them to your room, sir?

G : No, thanks. I'll wait here and collect them myself.

C : Okay, then please be seated over there.

(After a while)

Here you are. The charge comes to three dollars, sir.

G: Would you charge it to my room?

C : Yes, sir. May I have your name and room number, please?

G : Bill Jones, room 1205.

C : Would you please sign here?

G : Here you are.

C : Thank you, sir. Have a pleasant stay.

Key Points

* They will be ready within five minutes.

  5분 이내로 해드리겠습니다.

* Would you charge it to my room?

  그것을 손님의 객실로 요금을 부과할까요?

Dialogue Four

(***C*** : *Clerk* ***G*** : *Guest*)

(Asking to fax documents)

C : Good afternoon. Can I help you, ma'am?

G : Yes, please. I want to fax this document to my company in New York.

C : Please give me the document, then I'll fax it, ma'am.
Could you tell me your fax number, ma'am?

G : The number is 1-320-487-8277.

C : Okay. Just a minute, please.
(After a while)
I sent your fax, ma'am. Here's your document. Please confirm with the receiver that they got your fax.

G : Yes, thanks a lot.

C : You're welcome. Have a nice day, ma'am.

Key Points

* Could you tell me your fax number?
  팩스번호를 말씀해 주시겠습니까?
* Please confirm with the receiver that they got your fax.
  손님의 팩스를 받았는지를 수신자에게 확인하여 주십시오.

Dialogue Five

(***C*** : *Clerk*   ***G*** : *Guest*)

(Asking for translation)

C : Good morning, sir. Can I help you?

G : Yes. May I ask a favor of you?

C : How can I help you, sir?

G : I need to translate these papers into Korean.

C : Certainly, sir. Shall I see them, sir?

G : Okay, here they are. How many hours will it take to be translated?

C : About an hour, sir.

G : Oh, that's great. These are very important papers for this afternoon's meeting. Then I'll be back here in an hour.

C : See you then, sir.

Key Points

* May I ask a favor of you?
  부탁드릴 말이 있는데요.
* How many hours will it take to be translated?
  번역하는데 몇 시간이 걸릴까요?

■ Language Choices 1

1. Would you mail this letter express, please?
2. Would you post this letter by registered mail, please?
3. Can you send this document by DHL, please?
4. Would you please fax these papers for me?

Practice

Step 1. Use the words or phrases in the box to fill in the spaces below.

bring / transfer / seated / document / translate / be back / send / happy / copy / confirm

1. I'll be ___________ to send it for you.
2. I'll ___________ here in an hour.
3. Shall I ___________ it to your room account?
4. Shall I ___________ them to your room?
5. Please be ___________ over there.
6. Please ___________ with the receiver that they got your fax.
7. I want to fax this ___________ to my company in New York.
8. I need to ___________ these papers into Korean.
9. I'll ___________ it by DHL.
10. I'd like to ___________ these documents.

Step 2. Discuss with your partner or group.

1. Why is prompt service important for business customers?
2. How are business customer's needs different from tourist's needs?

Reading

Read the following story and answer the questions with five minutes.

■ Business Center Service

Business centers provide customers with a personally tailored business service. The aim of business centers is to improve the service quality using modern technology, facilitating more efficient ways in personal business assistance. In commercial hotels, the priority of operating a business center is to provide the most convenience for guests during their business trips. However, the number of business centers has increased recently even among resort hotels, the reason being that this can provide a concept of recreation and help refuel customers as they work.

Business centers provide various services as follows: firstly, they transmit the business of customers; secondly, they actively involve themselves in assisting with a customers' personal business; thirdly, they maintain facilities and keep mechanical equipment clean; and lastly, they oversee all gathered information as well as writing their business reports.

Questions For Discussion

1. What is the purpose of operating a business center?
2. What concept was introduced in resort hotels with the operation of additional business centers?
3. What services are offered in a business centre?

Role Play of Business Center Clerk

1. Do role plays of asking to mail a letter or to fax documents.
2. Do role plays of asking for translation or photocopying.

Lesson 9 Duty Manager Service

- Dialogue One
- Dialogue Two
- Dialogue Three
- Dialogue Four

Dialogue One

(***M***: *Duty Manager* ***G1***: *Guest*, ***G2***: *Guest*)

(Dealing with complaints on excessive noise)

M: Hello. This is the duty manager. What can I do for you?

G1: I'd like to sleep as I'm so tired from traveling, but I can't sleep well because of the noise from room 633.

M: I'm really sorry for the inconvenience. I'll take care of the problem right away, sir.

G1: Thank you.

M: Hello. Is this room 633, sir?

G2: Yes. What's the matter?

M: This is the duty manager. There's been a complaint about the noise level. We have to ask you to keep the volume down. We'll appreciate it if you could cooperate.

G2: Really? I'm very sorry if we were disturbing her.

M: That's alright, sir.

Key Points

* I'm really sorry for the inconvenience.
  불편하게 해서 정말 미안합니다.
* I'll take care of the problem right away.
  곧 그 문제를 처리해 드리겠습니다.
* We'll appreciate it if you could cooperate.
  손님께 협조하여 주신다면 감사하겠습니다.

Dialogue Two

(***M*** : *Duty Manager* ***G*** : *Guest*)

(Asking to restore misplaced possessions)

M : Hello, this is the duty manager's desk. May I help you?

G : Sure. This is Mr. Green. I already checked out from room 806 one hour ago. I lost a new watch that I bought for my wife. I think I left it in my room.

M : Okay. I'll check with the room maid right now, Mr. Green. How can I get in touch with you?

G : I'll call you again after 20 minutes.

M : Okay.

(After a while)

G : Hello, can I speak to the duty manager?

M : This is the duty manager's desk.

G : This is Mr. Green. I called 20 minutes ago.

M : Our room maid has found your watch in your room, Mr. Green.

G : Oh! That's wonderful. Thanks a lot.

M : You're welcome. How can I return it to you, Mr. Green?

G : I'll be there after 30 minutes.

M : Good. I'll wait for you at my desk, Mr. Green.

G : Thank you so much.

Key Points

* I'll check with the room maid right now.
  지금 당장 룸메이드에게 확인하겠습니다.
* Our room maid has found your watch in your room.
  룸메이드가 객실에서 손님의 시계를 찾아 놓았습니다.
* How can I return it to you? 손님께 어떻게 그것을 돌려드릴 수 있을까요?

Dialogue Three

(***M***: *Duty Manager* ***G***: *Guest*)

(Dealing with a misplaced key)

M: Good morning. What can I help you with, ma'am?

G: I forgot my card key. Can you please open the door for me?

M: I'm very sorry, ma'am. You need to get a new one from the front desk clerk. It's for your protection. What's your room number?

G: It's room 928.

M: This way please, ma'am. I'll give the key.

G: Thanks for helping me out.

M: My pleasure.

Key Points

* You need to get a new one from the front desk clerk.
  프런트데스크 직원으로부터 새로운 것을 받으십시오.
* It's for your protection. 손님의 보호를 위해서입니다.
* Thanks for helping me out. 도와주신 것에 감사합니다.

Dialogue Four

(***M***: *Duty Manager* ***G***: *Guest*)

(Dealing with sudden patients)

M: The duty manager's desk. May I help you?

G: Yes, please. My wife doesn't feel well. Is there a house doctor in the hotel?

M: Yes. but I'm really sorry our house doctor is not available at this time. What seems to be the trouble, sir?

G: Well, she has a little pain in her stomach.

M: Would you like to go to the hospital immediately, sir?

G: Yes, please.

M: There is a hospital near here, sir. I'll be waiting for you in the lobby. And I'll have a taxi ready.

(After a while)

This is the road map, sir. Please show this to the taxi driver.

G: Thank you so much.

M: You're welcome, sir.

Key Points 

* I'm really sorry our house doctor is not available at this time.
  병원 입주 의사는 지금 이용할 수 없어서 죄송합니다.
* What seems to be the trouble? 어디가 아프십니까?
* Please show this to the taxi driver.
  택시 운전사에게 이것을 보여주십시오.

■ Language Choices 1

1. Is there a doctor in the hotel?
2. Is there a drugstore in the hotel?

■ Language Choices 2

1. I'm suffering from a bad stomach.
2. He has a little pain in his stomach.
3. I have a stomachache.
4. He has a sharp pain in the head.
5. I have a fever.
6. I have a headache.
7. He doesn't feel well.

Practice

Step 1. Use the words or phrases in the box to fill in the spaces below.

house doctor / complaint / check / were disturbing / need to / available / sleep / get / return

1. I'm very sorry if we ___________ her.
2. There's been a ___________ about the noise level.
3. You ___________ get a new one from the front desk clerk.
4. I'll ___________ with the room maid right now.
5. Is there a ___________ in the hotel?
6. How can I ___________ in touch with you?
7. How can I ___________ it to you?
8. I'm really sorry our house doctor is not at this ___________ time.
9. I can't ___________ well because of the noise from room 633.

Step 2. Discuss with your partner or group.

1. A customer reports that she has lost her passport. What is your advice?

Reading

Read the following story and answer the questions with five minutes.

■ Duty Manager

Duty managers act as a general manager during night shifts when they are absent. The role of the duty manager includes managing business operations on the whole, performing tasks associated with customer demands, and handling complaints and carrying out nightly business operations.

Duty managers are scheduled on 24 hours a day and offer all necessary resources for the comfort of VIPs and other customers. When an accident occurs in the hotel, duty managers must contact emergency services, evacuate all residents, protect the hotel's property from burglary, maintain nobility of the hotel, and report necessary misconduct of employees. The duty manager also supervises the frontline staff such as security, doormen and bellmen, as well as handles lost items and manages storage. Furthermore, duty managers must confront unruly guests who lack manners and displease the public and have them removed from the hotel.

Questions For Discussion

1. Why does a hotel need a duty manager?
2. Who plays the role of general manager when he/she is absent?
3. Why should duty managers confront and remove guests who act out and cause disturbance to the public?

Role Play of Duty Manager

1. Do a role play of the duty manager dealing with a complaint on excessive noise.
2. Do a role play of dealing with misplaced possessions and a role play of dealing with a locked-in key.
3. Do a role play of dealing with sudden patients in the hotel room.

PART 2

Housekeeping Service

Lesson 1 Housekeeper Service

- Introduction
- Dialogue One
- Dialogue Two
- Dialogue Three
- Dialogue Four
- Dialogue Five
- Dialogue Six
- Dialogue Seven

Introduction

The department of Housekeeping has responsibilities for cleaning and maintaining guest rooms, and assisting the front office to allocate appropriate guest rooms for customers. For example, housekeepers are in charge of room maintenance whereas room maids have various tasks such as cleaning rooms, and managing a small bar, and the hotel's lost & found. Lastly, the laundry department must handle all laundry requests from customers.

Since the room itself is one of the most important products of the hotel, its maintenance should become the central and essential focus. Hotel rooms are vital commodities, and thus controlling room quality has a crucial impact on increasing sales. The rooms must feel to a customer like a "home away from home", and therefore should always be maintained a clean and delicate manner.

Dialogue One

(***H***: *Housekeeper* ***G***: *Guest*)

(Dealing with an additional items request)

G: Hello. Is this housekeeping?

H: Yes, this is housekeeping. Can I help you, sir?

G: Yes. I need an extra bed, two more pillows and an extra blanket. Could you send them to my room?

H: All right, sir. Do you need anything else, sir?

G: No, that's all.

H: May I have your room number, sir?

G: Room 1327.

H: I'll send a room maid up them to you right away, sir.

G: I appreciate it.

H: You're welcome, sir.

Key Points 

* Do you need anything else? 또 다른 어떤 것이 필요하십니까?

* I'll send a room maid up them to you right away.
곧바로 룸메이드에게 그것들을 보내겠습니다.

Dialogue Two

(***H***: *Housekeeper* ***G***: *Guest*)

(Asking for additional face towels and blankets)

H: Housekeeping. What can I help you with?

G: This is room 1319. Could you get me one more face towel and an extra blanket?

H: Yes, sir. Anything else?

G: There is no soap left. Please give me some soap.

H: We'll send them to your room 1319 right away, sir.

G: I'd appreciate it.

H: Sorry for the inconvenience, sir. Have a nice stay.

Key Points 

* Could you get me one more face towel? 페이스타월 하나 더 주시겠습니까?

* We'll send them to your room right away.
곧바로 그것들을 손님의 룸으로 보내드리겠습니다.

Dialogue Three

(***H***: *Housekeeper* ***G***: *Guest*)

(Asking for additional towels and hangers)

H: Good evening, This is housekeeping. May I help you?

G: Sure. This is Mr. Smith in room 1211. I need a towel and two more hangers.

H: What kind of towel do you want, ma'am?

G: I'd like to have a face towel.

H: Is there anything else, ma'am?

G: Um, my room is not warm enough.

H: There is a heating controller on the wall.

G: It's still cold even though I adjusted it higher.

H: I'll send the housekeeper up right away.

G: Thank you. I'll wait.

H: Our room maid will bring them to your room 1211 in five minutes.

G: Thank you so much.

Key Points

* What kind of towel do you want?
  무슨 종류의 타월을 원하십니까?
* There is a heating controller on the wall.
  벽에 히팅 조절기가 있습니다.

Dialogue Four

(***H***: *Housekeeper* ***G***: *Guest*)

(Asking for room cleaning)

H: Housekeeping, may I help you?

G: Yes, this is room 1121. I need my room cleaned up because I'll be going out now. I'll be back around 1:30 p.m.

H: All right. A room maid will be there soon, sir.

G: By the way, I have many papers on the desk.
Don't let her touch the papers, please. I'm still working on them.

H: Certainly, sir. We never move them, sir.

G: And I need some more stationery. Please send it them to me. That's all.

H: Sure. Thank you very much for calling, sir.

Key Points 

* A room maid will be there soon.
  룸메이드가 곧 거기에 도착할 것입니다.
* Don't let her touch the papers, please.
  서류들은 만지지 않도록 시켜주십시오.
* We'll never move them.
  우리는 그것들을 그대로 둘 것입니다.

Dialogue Five

(*H*: *Housekeeper* *G*: *Guest*)

(Asking for a table or heating)

H: Good evening, housekeeping. How can I help you?

G: This is room 1223. I have to work in my room.

The desk in my room doesn't have enough space. And I need a table for my work. Can you bring a table to my room?

H: Sure. We'll bring a table immediately, sir.

G: Thank you.

H: Would you like anything else?

G: I feel a little cold. The room isn't warm enough.

H: There is a thermostat on the wall. Did you properly adjust it, sir?

G: No, I didn't.

H: Please wait for fifteen minutes after adjusting the thermostat.

I think it'll get warmer and warmer.

G: You certainly take good care of your guests.

H: It's my pleasure to be of service.

Key Points

* The room isn't warm enough.

  객실이 따뜻하지 않습니다.

* Did you properly adjust it?

  그것을 적당하게 조절했습니까?

* I think it'll get warmer and warmer.

  점점 따뜻하게 될 것으로 생각합니다.

Dialogue Six

(***H***: *Housekeeper* ***G***: *Guest*)

(Dealing with a faulty TV set)

H: (Knocking at door) Hello.

G: Who is it?

H: Housekeeper, ma'am. May I come in?

G: Come right in, please.

H: Did you call housekeeping to fix your television, ma'am?

G: Yes. I'd like to watch TV, but my television hasn't worked since last night.

H: Shall I turn it on, ma'am?

G: Sure.

H: I think we'll have an engineer look at this television set.

G: Okay. Please send an engineer up right away.

H: Yes, ma'am. Wait a few minutes, please.

Key Points

* Did you call the housekeeping to fix your television?
  하우스키핑에 텔레비전을 수리하도록 전화했습니까?
* Shall I turn it on?
  그것을 켜도 될까요?
* I think we'll have an engineer look at this television set.
  기술자에게 이 텔레비전을 돌보도록 하여야 할 것으로 생각됩니다.

Dialogue Seven

(*H*: *Housekeeper* *G*: *Guest*)

(Dealing with a broken thermostat)

H: This is the housekeeper, sir. May I come in?

G: Yes, come on in, please. I need to be warm enough because I have a terrible cold. I tried to adjust the thermostat on the wall, but I couldn't. And I want to take a bath, but there's no hot water.

H: I think there is something wrong. I'll have our maintenance man fix your thermostat.

G: All right.

H: I'll call him right now. I'll ask him to come up here in a few minutes. He'll fix it immediately.

G: Thank you. I'll wait for him.

H: I'm sorry to have you suffer from the inconvenience, sir. And if there is any discomfort while you stay here, please call us again.

Key Points

* I think there is something wrong.
  무엇인가 잘못되었다고 생각한다.
* I'll have our maintenance man fix your thermostat.
  우리 보수 담당원에게 온도 조절장치를 고치도록 시킬 것입니다.
* If there is any discomfort while you stay here, please call us again.
  당신이 체류하는 동안에 불편한 것이 있다면, 다시 전화해 주십시오.

■ Language Choices 1

1. I need a table for my work.
2. Can you bring me a towel and an extra bed?
3. Can I have an extra pillow and two more hangers?
4. I want to have one more blanket.
5. Will you get me a toothbrush?

■ Language Choices 2

1. We'll send them to your room.
2. We'll send a room maid up with it.
3. The room maid will bring it right up.
4. We'll have a room maid send to you right away.
5. Our room maid will be there in five minutes.

■ Language Choices 3

1. Would you make up my room 605?
2. Would you send a room maid to my room 612?
3. Could you clean up the room immediately?
4. I need my room cleaned.
5. Please have a room maid come to my room 712 because the room is just a mess.

■ Language Choices 4

1. The television set is out of order.
2. The phone is broken.
3. The thermostat doesn't work.
4. The picture isn't clear.
5. There is something wrong with the thermostat.
6. The water in the toilet is overflowing.
7. The toilet is stopped up.

■ Language Choices 5

1. I'll send the repairman to fix the air-conditioner.
2. I'll inform our maintenance man to fix the TV.
3. I'll ask an engineer to fix this thermostat.
4. I'll have the maintenance man fix the heating controller.

Practice

Step 1. Use the words or phrases in the box to fill in the spaces below.

get / heating / need / send / adjusted / bring / fix / have / cleaned

1. There is a ___________ controller on the wall.
2. I ___________ a towel and two more hangers.
3. Our room maid will ___________ them to your room 1211 in five minutes.
4. Could you ___________ me one more face towel and an extra blanket?
5. Did you call the housekeeping to ___________ your television?
6. The desk in my room doesn't ___________ enough space.
7. It's still cold even though I ___________ it higher.
8. I'll ___________ a room maid up them to you right away.
9. I need my room ___________ up because I'll be going out now.

Reading

Read the following story and answer the questions with five minutes.

■ Housekeeper Service

Housekeepers are responsible for the safety of their customers and their belongings, and thus require the ability to act quickly in emergency situations. In addition, housekeepers must immediately notify the hotel office about any need for urgent repairs that have significant impact upon a guest's stay at the hotel, and in the end confirm that the problem has been completely fixed.

All housekeeping keys are stored in the office. When using a housekeeping key, the time of use and the housekeeper's signature should be written down on a key sign book. Most importantly, a key cannot be lent to others or used for purposes other to fulfil a particular task. In this regard, housekeeping keys should be treated and managed as an invaluable asset.

After using a key, the time and the signature must be recorded in the key sign book and the key must be replaced at its designated location and confirmed with the office clerk.

Questions For Discussion

1. Does a housekeeper need to check the room from a customer's perspective?
2. Why do housekeepers need to confirm whether or not repairs are completed before they can end their shifts?
3. Can housekeepers consider housekeeping keys as a second life (invaluable assets)?
4. Explain how housekeepers must manage the key.

Role Play of Housekeeper

1. Do a role play of the housekeeper dealing with requests on an extra bed, pillow, blanket, table and hanger.
2. Do a role play of the housekeeper dealing with a request on room cleaning.
3. Do a role play of the housekeeper dealing with a malfunctioning TV set and thermostat.

Lesson 2 Room Maid Service

Dialogue One

(*M*: *Room Maid* *G*: *Guest*)

(Asking to delay room cleaning)

G: (Knocking at the door) Who is it?

M: Good morning. This is the room maid, sir. If you don't mind, I'd like to clean the room now.

G: Oh! No. I'm so busy. I have to do my paperwork.

M: I'm very sorry to have disturbed you, sir. What time would be convenient for you, sir?

G: Let's see. Would it be convenient for you to clean my room at around 11:00 o'clock?

M: No problem, sir.

Key Points 

* If you don't mind, I'd like to clean the room now.
  괜찮으시다면, 지금 객실을 청소하고자 합니다.
* What time would be convenient for you? 몇 시가 편리합니까?

Dialogue Two

(*M*: *Room Maid* *G*: *Guest*)

(Making an item delivery)

M: (The room maid knocks on the door) Hello. This is the room maid, sir.

G: Wait a moment, please.

M: Yes, sir.

G: Come in, please.

M: I've brought two face towels and a pillow you asked for, sir.

G: I appreciate your kindness.

M: Would you like anything else, sir?

G: Well. Could you give me some water in the pitcher?

M: Yes, I'll bring it to you immediately, sir.

G: Thank you so much.

Key Points 

* I've brought two face towels and a pillow you asked for.
  손님이 요청한 타월 2개와 베개를 가지고 왔습니다.
* I'll bring it to you immediately. 곧바로 그것을 가지고 가겠습니다.

Dialogue Three

(***M***: *Room Maid* ***G***: *Guest*)

(Room cleaning)

M: (knocking on the door) Room Maid. May I come in to clean the room?

G: Yes. Please come in. I need my room made up.

M: I'd have to change the new bed sheet, two towels, two pillows cases, ... and fill the water pitcher, sir.

G: Okay. How long will it take to clean?

M: Maybe it'll take about 30 minutes.

G: Please clean my room as soon as possible. I'm still working now.

M: Yes, I'll do it quickly.

G: I appreciate it.

M: Thanks a lot.

Key Points 

* I have to change a new bed sheet, two towels, two pillows cases, ... and fill the water pitcher, sir. 침대시트와 타월 두 개, 베개 커버 두 개를 바꾸겠습니다. 그리고 물을 채우겠습니다.
* Please clean my room as soon as possible. 가능한 빨리 해주십시오.

Dialogue Four

(***M***: *Room Maid* ***G***: *Guest*)

(Asking not to touch papers)

M: Good morning, sir. May I help you?

G: Yes. I'm going out for a while. Please make up room 523.

M: Yes, sir.

G: I have left many papers on the desk. Don't touch the papers on the desk, please. I have to work again after I come back. Those papers are very important for tomorrow's meeting.

M: Yes, I'll take care of your papers, sir. Do you need anything else?

G: Please fill more ice water in the kettle.

M: Okay.

Key Points 

* Please make up the room. 객실청소를 하여 주십시오.
* Don't touch the papers on the desk, please. 책상 위의 서류를 만지지 마세요.
* I'll take care of your papers. 서류를 조심할게요.

Dialogue Five

(***M*** : *Room Maid* ***G*** : *Guest*)

(Adjusting the thermostat)

M : (Knocking on the door) This is housekeeping. Good evening, sir.

G : Come in, please. The thermostat needs to be adjusted.

M : I'll adjust the thermostat as you requested.

G : Oh, that's good. I'm still not warm enough. I've had a cold.

M : I adjusted it to the highest setting.

G : Thanks a lot.

M : It's my pleasure. Have a comfortable stay, sir.

Key Points 

* I'll adjust the thermostat as you requested.
  요청하신대로 온도조절기를 조절하겠습니다.
* I adjusted it to the highest setting.
  가장 높은 온도로 조절해 드리겠습니다.

■ Language Choices 1

1. I'd like to make up your room now, ma'am.
2. I'm going to clean up the room.
3. I want to clean your room now.
4. I'd like to clean the room.
5. May I clean your room now?
6. May I come in to clean the room?

■ Language Choices 2

1. The papers on the desk aren't finished.
2. Don't move my documents on the table, please.
3. Don't touch the papers, please.

■ Language Choices 3

1. I've brought the face towel you asked for.
2. I'll clean your room as you required.
3. I'll adjust the thermostat you asked.

Practice

Step 1. Use the words or phrases in the box to fill in the spaces below.

work / clean / give / take / clean / convenient / adjust / setting

1. I'll __________ care of your papers.
2. I have to __________ again after I come back.
3. Would it be __________ for you to clean my room at around 11:00 o'clock?
4. Could you __________ me some water in the pitcher?
5. I'll __________ the thermostat as you requested.
6. Please __________ my room as soon as possible.
7. I'd like to __________ the room now.
8. I adjusted it to the highest __________.

Reading

Read the following story and answer the questions with five minutes.

■ Room Maid Service

Room maids' primary tasks are to offer a comforting and clean environment, polite services, and convenient facilities. Thus, Room maids have a significant responsibility in determining room quality, and handling lost and found items. Room maids must not open guest doors until their identification is verified. In addition, they must not use the telephone in the room or receive any incoming calls while cleaning. On the other hand, linen or towels should not be utilized as cleaning products.

When the 'Do not disturb' sign is hung on the door handle, the room maid must not knock on the door. Before entering the room, they must press the chime bell first, then, confirming there is no response, open the door using the key. They must check the linen of the bed and the bathroom, and neatly set up any unused linen.

Questions For Discussion

1. What kind of services is mainly offered to customers by room maid?
2. What kind of procedures should room maid follow when they enter the room?
3. How should room maids handle any unused linen?

Role Play of Room Maid

1. Do a role play of the housekeeper dealing with a request on room cleaning and room cleaning delay.
2. Do a role play of the housekeeper delivering requested items and dealing with request on thermostat readjustment.

Lesson 3 Lost & Found Service

- Dialogue One
- Dialogue Two
- Dialogue Three

1 Dialogue One

(***H***: *Housekeeper* ***G***: *Guest*)

(Mailing misplaced possessions to the checked-out guest)

G: Hello, is this the housekeeping office?

H: Yes. Can I help you?

G: This is Mr. Smith. I just checked out of room 831. My wife has lost her ring. Perhaps she dropped it somewhere in the room. Have you seen it perhaps?

H: Ah! Mr. Smith. You are lucky. It's been found by our room maid in your room. And we're keeping it at the Lost and Found. I think we have your wife's ring.

G: Oh, good. She will be very happy. Well. How can I get it? I'm calling from N.Y.

H: Don't worry about that, Mr. Smith. We have your home address. We'll send it to you by registered mail tomorrow morning.

G: I'm very glad you can do that for me. You're very kind. We'll always remember what you have done for us.

H: It's my pleasure. Have a nice day and I hope to see you again in the future.

Key Points

* Have you seen it perhaps? 혹시 그것을 보았습니까?
* It's been found by our room maid in your room.
  객실에서 룸메이드가 발견했습니다.
* We're keeping it at the Lost and Found.
  분실물 보관실에서 그것을 보관하고 있습니다.

Dialogue Two

(***H***: *Housekeeper* ***G***: *Guest*)

(Asking to retrieve the misplaced possession)

G: Excuse me, is this housekeeping?

H: Yes. May I help you, sir?

G: Yes, please. I've lost my watch. I'd like to check it.
I think I've left my watch on the desk.

H: Oh, that's too bad. May I have your name and room number, sir?

G: Mr. Brown in room 925. Could it be in your Lost and Found?

H: I'm sorry. There have been no Lost and Found items reported this morning, Mr. Brown. But we'll check the room right away. We'll do our best to find your watch, Mr. Brown.
(After a while)
I'm sorry, but we couldn't find it in your room. Did you look through all of your belongings, Mr. Brown?

G: Yes, I did. I still can't find it. I have to find it. Did you check on the night table?

H: Yes. When did you notice that your watch was missing?

G: I noticed it when I got to my office.

H: Where did you go last night, Mr. Brown?

G: I went to the fitness center last night.

H: We'll check the fitness center, Mr. Brown. Please fill out this "Lost Article Report". If it's found, we'll call you.

G: I'll be waiting for your call.

Key Points

* Did you find all of your belongings?
  소지품을 모두 뒤져보았습니까?
* When did you notice that your watch was missing?
  시계가 없다는 것을 언제 알았습니까?
* Please fill out this "Lost Article Report".
  "분실신고서"를 작성하여 주십시오.

■ Language Choices 1

1. Maybe I dropped my watch some place in the room.
2. I've left my ring on the desk.
3. I think I must have left my handbag in my room.
4. I lost my purse in the room.

■ Language Choices 2

1. Our room maid found the ring by our room maid.
2. We've searched for the purse through all of your room, but we couldn't find it.
3. The purse was found by the room maid.

Practice 

Step 1. Use the words or phrases in the box to fill in the spaces below.

registered / send / dropped / done / worry / left / found / Lost and Found / notice

1. I think I've ___________ my watch on the desk.
2. Don't ___________ about that.
3. We'll ___________ it to you by registered mail tomorrow morning.
4. It's been ___________ by our room maid in your room.
5. We'll send it to you by ___________ mail tomorrow morning.
6. Perhaps she ___________ it somewhere in the room.
7. We'll always remember what you have __________ for us.
8. There have been no ___________ items reported this morning.
9. When did you ___________ that your watch was missing?

Step 2. Discuss with your partner or group.

1. Did the housekeeper provide good service? How?
2. Have you ever lost something valuable? How did you feel?

☆ Remember how you felt when you help your guest.

Reading

Read the following story and answer the questions with five minutes.

■ Lost & Found Service

The Lost & found department should keep, handle, and return customers' lost items safely. When they receive an inquiry about a customer's lost & found items either by phone or by person, they must not inform them carelessly. All frontline employees should recognize accurate procedures about handling their lost & found items.

The main tasks of Lost & Found representatives are to handle the lost & found items and maintain their cleanliness. Upon receipt of lost goods, they must find out the customer's contact details then try to reach the customer as quickly as possible. If there is no way to contact the customer, they should keep the lost items for a certain period of time under their own responsibility, then, following the regulations, transfer to other service departments. Before delivering these items, they must record specific features of the lost item such as color, style, kind, and quality.

Questions For Discussion

1. Why do you think the lost items should be documented when they are kept?
2. What do you think about the main role of the Lost & Found representative?
3. If there is no way to contact the right customer who lost their items, how should this issue be resolved?

Role Play of Housekeeper(Lost & Found)

1. Do a role play of mailing a guest's misplaced possession when the guest calls.
2. Do a role play of the housekeeper and guest when visited at the front desk again to collect the misplaced possession.

Lesson 4 Laundry Service

- Dialogue One
- Dialogue Two
- Dialogue Three
- Dialogue Four

Dialogue One

(***C***: *Laundry Clerk* ***G***: *Guest*)

(Taking an order for laundry on the phone)

C: Hello, this is laundry. May I help you?

G: Yes. I have some laundry. Can you send someone over to my room?

C: Yes. May I have your name and the room number, sir?

G: Mr. Brown and the room number is 1109.

C: A valet will pick them up right away. Please wait a moment, Mr. Brown.
(After a while)
This is laundry service. May I come in?

G: Yes, come on in, please. I have some shirts and underwear to be washed. If I send out my laundry now, when can I get them back?

C: We can make them ready until 8:00 tomorrow morning, sir. If you want a quick service, you have to pay a 50% extra charge.

G: That will be fine. I need them by 8:30 tomorrow morning.

C: You can get them back by regular service at 8:00 tomorrow morning, sir.

G: Oh! Good. I'd like it by regular service.

C: Certainly, sir. I'll pick them up right now.

G: OK. Thank you.

Key Points

* Can you send someone over to my room?
  객실에 누군가를 보낼 수 있습니까?
* If you want a quick service, you have to pay a 50% extra charge.
  만일 빠른 서비스를 받기를 원한다면, 50% 특별요금을 지불하여야 합니다.
* You can get them back by regular service at 8:00 tomorrow morning.
  손님께서는 내일 아침 8시에 보통 서비스로 그것들을 제공받을 수 있습니다.

Dialogue Two

(**C**: *Laundry Clerk* **G**: *Guest*)

(Getting the laundry to the guest)

C: (knocking at the door) Laundry service. May I help you?

G: Yes, I have some laundry. My room number is 728.

C: A valet will pick them up right away.
(After a while)
May I come in to pick up your laundry?

G: Of course. I'd like to have some shirts cleaned and pressed. I want them to be delivered by tomorrow evening.

C: Sure. You'll get them back by tomorrow evening, sir. Maybe we can deliver them by five p.m. tomorrow.

G: That's good.

C: Excuse me. Please fill out this laundry slip, sir.

G: Sure. Here you are.

C: I'll check them to make sure.

G: Is that correct?

C: Yes, that's correct. I'll bring it by then, sir. Thank you so much.

Key Points 

* May I come in to pick up your laundry?
  손님의 세탁물을 가지러 왔는데 들어가도 될까요?
* I want them to be delivered by tomorrow evening.
  내일 저녁까지 배달되기를 바랍니다.
* I'll check them to make sure. 확인하기 위해 그것들을 점검하겠습니다.

Dialogue Three

(***C***: *Laundry Clerk* ***G***: *Guest*)

(Asking to remove stains on the laundry)

C: Laundry service. May I come in?

G: Come on in, please. I want to get the laundry done.
By the way, there are a lot of stains here. Can you take these stains off completely?

C: We'll do our best to get the stains out, sir.

G: Okay. Please don't rub these shirts too much to remove the stains.

C: Yes, you don't have to worry about that, sir. I'll be mindful of that, sir.
Please leave them to us. What is this material, sir?

G: Pure silk and be careful not to scorch these shirts.

C: Yes, we'll be careful, sir.

G: How long will it take?

C: You can get them by 3 o'clock tomorrow afternoon.

G: All right.

C: Here's the laundry slip. Please list the quantity of each article on this slip.
Please sign here for them, sir. Thank you very much.

Key Points 

* Can you take these stains off completely?
  얼룩들을 완전히 제거할 수 있습니까?
* Please don't rub these shirts too much to remove the stains.
  얼룩들을 제거하기 위해 너무 많이 셔츠를 비비지 마십시오.
* Please list the quantity of each article on this slip.
  전표에 각각 품목의 수량을 기입하여 주십시오.

Dialogue Four

(**C** : *Laundry Clerk* **G** : *Guest*)

(Delivering the laundry to the guest)

C : Good morning. This is laundry. May I help you?

G : My room number is 825. Can I have some laundry done?

C : Yes, sir. What kind of laundry do you have?

G : I have two shirts. Can you send someone to my room?

C : Yes, sir. I'll send a valet to your room right away, sir.
(After a while)
Hello, this is laundry. May I come in?

G : Yes, come on in, please. This is my laundry. I need them by tomorrow morning. Can I get them back at that time?

C : Yes. We can deliver them by tomorrow morning, sir.

G : Thanks.

C : It's my pleasure.
(Next day morning)
Hello.

G : Who is it?

C : Laundry service. May I come in, sir?

G : Yes, come in, please.

C : I've brought your shirts, sir.
Shall I put them in the closet?

G : Yes, please. Let me see. Did you take off the stains completely?

C : Yes, would you please check your shirts, sir?

G : Yes, it looks good.

C : Here's the laundry slip, sir. Could you please sign here?

G : Sure.

Key Points

* What kind of laundry do you have?
무슨 종류의 세탁물이 있습니까?
* Shall I put them in the closet?
옷장에 넣어둘까요?
* Did you take off the stains completely?
얼룩을 완전히 제거했습니까?

■ Language Choices 1

1. I have the laundry to be cleaned and pressed.
2. I'd like to have this suit dry cleaned and pressed.
3. I have some shirts that need pressing.
4. I need this laundry cleaned.
5. Can I have some laundry done?

■ Language Choices 2

1. We can have them ready by 8:00 tomorrow morning.
2. You can get it by 9:00 tomorrow morning.
3. You'll get it back by tomorrow afternoon.
4. We can deliver them tomorrow evening.

■ Language Choices 3

1. Can you get this spot out?
2. Can you remove these stains?
3. Can you take these stains completely off?

Practice

Step 1. Use the words or phrases in the box to fill in the spaces below.

fill out / delivered / take / send / valet / list / come in / pick / laundry

1. May I __________ to pick up your laundry?
2. I'll send a __________ to your room right away.
3. Can you __________ these stains off completely?
4. Please __________ this laundry slip.
5. Can you __________ someone over to my room?
6. I want them to be __________ by tomorrow evening.
7. Please __________ the quantity of each article on this slip.
8. A valet will __________ them up right away.
9. What kind of __________ do you have?

Reading

Read the following story and answer the questions with five minutes.

■ Laundry Service

The tasks of the Laundry department are to use their experience in professional laundering to quickly and hygienically deal with any laundry requests. Hotel laundry services must collect and launder requested laundry items immediately upon request to provide maximum convenience to customers. Also, the laundry service also should deliver customer apparel, as good as new, at the requested time of the customer.

The collected laundry items must be accurately divided into Pressing, Dry Cleaning or Washing, and then sent to the appropriate departments after tagging. If there are any errors found when checking the laundry, they should contact the laundry service manager, need his/her advice then proceed to fix the problem. All of the finalized laundry should be sent to the laundry service manager to arrange delivery back to each customer.

Questions For Discussion

1. Why does the laundry staff require professional skill and experiences?
2. Let's explain the procedure of the laundry service.
3. What should laundry service managers do when faced with an error in customers' laundry?

Role Play of Laundry Clerk

1. Do a role play of taking a laundry order and quick service.
2. Do a role play of being asked to remove stains on the laundry and delivering it.

PART 3

Food and Beverage Department

Restaurant Reservation Service

- Introduction
- Dialogue One
- Dialogue Two
- Dialogue Three
- Dialogue Four
- Dialogue Five

Introduction

Food & Beverage Department offers material and human services in order to sell food and beverage products. It is not simply providing restaurant services, but also offering the best products that meet various demands and satisfactions of customers. The fundamental differences between the white linen service of a hotel and many other restaurants are: firstly, a pleasant atmosphere; secondly, an optimal level of customer service; thirdly, hygiene and fresh supplies; and lastly, diversity in menu.

Depending on the size and scale of the kitchen or serving area, the number of restaurants differs in each hotel. The Food & Beverage service venues are consisted of grill, coffee shop, bar, lobby lounge, room service, banquet room, and club lounge. Particularly, the department of banquet is mainly responsible for sales, reservations, and banquet services.

Dialogue One

(***M***: *Manager* ***G***: *Guest*)

(Asking to make a reservation for dinner)

M: Good morning. River View. Can I help you?

G: Yes, please. What time do you open for dinner?

M: We open at 5:00 every evening and close at 10:00 p.m., sir.

G: Could I make a reservation for three people for this evening?

M: Yes, of course. And for what time would that be, sir?

G: We'll be there at about 7:00. Can you give me a quiet table, please?

M: Yes, your table is reserved to a quiet one. May I have your name, sir?

G : Jack Martin.

M : That's a table for three for this evening at 7 p.m. for Mr. Martin.

G : Yes, that's right.

M : Thank you for calling us. We'll be expecting you, Mr. Martin. Have a good day.

G : Thank you. Bye.

Key Points 

* For what time would that be, sir?
몇 시에 오실 것입니까?

* Can you give me a quiet table?
조용한 테이블을 줄 수 있습니까?

* That's a table for three for this evening at 7 p.m. for Mr. Martin.
마틴님을 위해 오늘 저녁 오후 7시에 3명 예약되었습니다.

Dialogue Two

(***C*** : *Captain* ***G*** : *Guest*)

(Asking to make a reservation for a luncheon)

C : Good morning. Seasons restaurant, Mr. Lee speaking. Can I help you?

G : Yes, what time do you open for lunch?

C : From 12 to 3, sir.

G : I'd like to book for lunch tomorrow.

C : For what time and for how many would that be, sir?

G : I want to reserve a table for five at one o'clock.

C : Fine! Who's booking, sir?

G : Bill Jones. I want to make a reservation for a table near a window.

C: Thank you, Mr. Jones. We'll arrange for a table near the window for five at 1:00 p.m. tomorrow. Your reservation for lunch tomorrow is confirmed, Mr. Jones. We look forward to seeing you then. Thank you for calling, Mr. Jones.

G: Thanks, bye.

Key Points 

* For what time and for how many would that be?
  몇 시에 몇 명이 오시겠습니까?
* We'll arrange for a table for five at 1:00 p.m. tomorrow.
  내일 오후 1시에 5명을 위한 테이블을 마련하겠습니다.
* We look forward to seeing you then. 그때 손님을 뵙겠습니다.

Dialogue Three

(***M***: *Manager* ***G***: *Guest*)

(Asking to make a reservation for party)

M: Rainbow restaurant, Miss Kim speaking. May I help you?

G: I've got a group of 20 persons. We want to reserve for dinner tomorrow evening.

M: Very well. May I have your name, sir?

G: Jonathan Thomas.

M: What time would you like the reservation, Mr. Thomas?

G: We'll be there at around 7:00 p.m.

M: That's good. May I have your telephone number, please?

G: 751～8277. We want tables near the window with a nice view.

M: Well. We'll have the tables by the window ready for you.

G: Thank you.

M : If you'd like to change or cancel, please call us, Mr. Thomas.

G : Sure.

M : Thank you for calling us. We'll be expecting you. Have a nice day.

Key Points 

* We want tables near the window with a nice view.
  전망이 좋은 창문 가까운 테이블을 원합니다.
* If you'd like to change or cancel, please call us.
  만일 변경이나 취소할 경우 우리에게 전화 바랍니다.

Dialogue Four

(***C*** : *Captain* ***G*** : *Guest*)

(Dealing with a guest when no table is available for reservation)

C : Good morning, Lakeside restaurant. How can I help you?

G : Do you have a table for five this evening at 7:00?

C : One moment, sir. Let me check the reservation list. I'm sorry, but we're full until eight o'clock this evening, sir.

G : Then, what time can we have a table available this evening?

C : Well. We'll have a table at eight-ten tonight, sir.

G : Okay, that'll be fine. Please give me a quiet table.

C : Yes, sir. Who's making the reservation, sir?

G : Mr. Thomson.

C : We'll book a table at eight-ten this evening and serve you then. We'll see you then.

G : Good-bye.

Key Points

* I'm sorry, but we're full until eight o'clock this evening.
  미안하지만, 오늘 저녁 8시까지는 예약이 완료되었습니다.
* We'll have a table at eight-ten tonight.
  8시 10분에 좌석이 있습니다.

Dialogue Five

(***M*** : *Manager* ***G*** : *Guest*)

(Asking to cancel the reserved table)

G : Is this Rose restaurant?

M : Yes, sir. May I help you?

G : I made a reservation for a table for three for lunch at noon today. But I am afraid I must cancel my reservation. I have to put it off to next time.

M : Who made the reservation, sir?

G : I made it under Mr. Cooper.

M : Thanks for letting us know in advance. I would like to have the chance to serve you in the future.

G : I hope so, too. Good-bye.

Key Points

* I'm afraid I made a reservation for a table for three for lunch at noon today, but I've got to cancel my reservation.
  오늘 12시에 점심을 위해 3명 예약한 것을 취소할까 합니다.
* Who made the reservation, sir? 손님, 누가 예약을 했습니까?
* I made it under Mr. Cooper.
  Mr. Cooper의 이름으로 예약이 되어 있습니다.
* Thanks for letting us know. 우리에게 알려 주셔서 감사합니다.

■ Language Choices 1

1. I'd like to reserve a table for two for dinner this evening.
2. I want to book a table for three for lunch tomorrow.
3. I'd like to make a reservation for a table for four for the dinner buffet at 7:00 this evening.
4. I'm calling to book a table for twelve for dinner.

■ Language Choices 2

1. For what day and time (do you want to book), sir?
2. What day and time would you like to reserve, sir?
3. For what time would that be, sir?
4. What day and time would you like to be served, sir?

■ Language Choices 3

1. How many people would there be in your party, sir?
2. For how many people, ma'am?
3. How many are in your party, sir?

■ Language Choices 4

1. Who's booking, sir?
2. Who's the reservation for, sir?
3. Who's making the reservation, ma'am?
4. What name is the reservation under, sir?

■ Language Choices 5

1. I'm sorry, we're booked for this evening.
2. I'm sorry, we're full on Sunday.
3. I'm sorry, we have no table at that time.
4. We're fully booked for dinner today.
5. I'm sorry, but we're full until eight o'clock this evening, sir.

Practice 

Step 1. Use the words or phrases in the box to fill in the spaces below.

like to / reservation / making / arrange / give / three / check / cancel

1. We'll ________ for a table near the window for five at 1:00 p.m. tomorrow.
2. That's a table for __________ for this evening at 7 p.m.
3. I'd __________ book for lunch tomorrow.
4. Let me __________ the reservation list.
5. Who's __________ the reservation?
6. I am afraid I must __________ my reservation.
7. Could I make the __________ for three people for this evening?
8. Can you __________ me a quiet table, please?

Step 2. Discuss with your partner.

1. Prepare a list of information you need from the guest when making a reservation.

Reading

Read the following story and answer the questions with five minutes.

■ Restaurant Reservation Service

If the phone rings, the staff must answer it as quickly as possible. Providing immediate responses for a reservation call is one of the fundamental manners of answering calls in restaurants. A customer generally begins to feel frustrated after three rings. When answering a call, the name of the hotel, restaurant, and receiver should politely be given first, then the staff should enquire about the name of the caller and their queries. If audio is hindered by poor connection or soft volume, the staff should ask the customer politely until they can confirm the request of the customer.

Particularly in restaurants, the booking date and time, and number of customers must be written down accurately and reconfirmed with the customer. For this, the staff must always be prepared with note paper and pen as to be able to write down anything important at any time. In addition, words should be spoken clearly and politely, and the volume, intonation, and speed of the speech must also be methodically considered.

Questions For Discussion

1. What is the principle mannerism when answering a call from a customer?
2. What must be said first when answering a call?
3. What must be said when answering reservation calls?
4. What factors must be considered when answering reservation calls?

Role Play of Restaurant Reservation Clerk

1. Do a role play of taking a table reservation for luncheon or dinner.
2. Do a role play of dealing with a guest when no table is available for reservation.

Lesson 2 Seating the Guest

Dialogue One

(***R***: *Receptionist* ***G***: *Guest*)

(Dealing with a guest visiting the restaurant without a reservation)

R: Good afternoon, sir. How are you today?

G: Just fine. Do you have a table available for three?

R: Do you have a reservation, sir?

G: No. We don't.

R: I'm sorry, sir. We don't have any tables available just now. But if you don't mind waiting, we can make a table for you in about 15 minutes. We should get a couple of free tables soon.

G: That's great.

R: Please wait here, sir. I'll call you just as soon as we are ready.
(After a while)
Your table is ready now, sir. We're very sorry for having kept you waiting for so long. I'll show you to your table. This way, please.

G: We'd like to have a window seat. Can we have that table by the window?

R: Sorry, sir. That table is reserved, but here's a nice table for three. How about this seat, sir?

G: That's fine. I appreciate your kindness.

R: I'll be right back to take your order. Here's your menu.

Key Points

* I'll call you just as soon as we are ready.
준비되자마자 곧 부르겠습니다.
* We're very sorry for having kept you waiting for so long.
오랫동안 기다리게 해서 미안합니다.
* That table is reserved, but here's a nice table for three.
저 테이블은 예약된 것이며, 여기에 3명에게는 좋은 테이블이 있습니다.

Dialogue Two

(***R***: *Receptionist*　　***G***: *Guest*)

(Escorting a reserved guest to their table)

R: Good afternoon, sir. Welcome to our restaurant. May I help you, sir?

G: Yes, I'm trying to find the cafeteria. Could you tell me where it is?

R: This is the cafeteria.

G: I'm Joly Lewis. We reserved a table for three for our lunch.

R: Wait a moment, please. I'll check it, Mr. Lewis. You reserved a table for three people. Please come with me. This is your seat.

G: Excuse me, we'd like a table by the window. Would you mind if we sit at that table by the window?

R: Please take a seat, Mr. Lewis.

G: Thank you.

R: Your waiter will be with you in a moment.
Enjoy your dinner, sir.

Key Points

* Would you mind if we sit at that table by the window?
  창가 저 테이블에 우리가 앉아도 괜찮겠습니까?
* Your waiter will be with you in a moment.
  잠시 후 웨이터가 올 것입니다.

Dialogue Three

(***W***: *Waiter, Waitress* ***G***: *Guest*)

(Escorting a guest asking for a non-smoking table)

W: Good evening, sir. You seem to be having a good evening.

G: Yes, very good. We need a table for four.

W: Do you have a reservation, sir?

G: No, we don't.

W: Do you have any seat preference, sir?

G: We'd like a table by the window.

W: Would you like smoking or non-smoking, sir?

G: Non smoking.

W: All right, sir. Would you like to sit by the lakeside?

G: Sure. We'd love to.

W: I'll take you to the beautiful lakeside seat by the window. This way, please. This seat commands a fine view of the lakeside. How is this table, sir?

G: Oh! It's beautiful. Thank you.

W: You're welcome. I'm glad you like it here. A waitress will be with you in a moment, sir. Enjoy your dinner, sir.

Key Points

* You seem you're having a good evening.
  매우 기분 좋으신 것처럼 보입니다.
* This seat commands a fine view of the lakeside.
  이 좌석은 호숫가로 전망이 좋습니다.
* Would you like smoking or non-smoking, sir?
  흡연석과 금연석 가운데 어느 것으로 하겠습니까?

■ Language Choices 1

1. I need a table for two.
2. Do you have a table for two?
3. Do you have a table available for three?

■ Language Choices 2

1. Would you come with me, please?
2. Would you please follow me?
3. This way, please.
4. Come this way, please.

■ Language Choices 3

1. Do you have a seat by the window?
2. Do you have a table with a fine view for me?
3. Do you want to take a seat by the window?
4. I'd like a table with a good view of the lakeside.
5. I want a table near the window with a nice view.

Practice

Step 1. Use the words or phrases in the box to fill in the spaces below.

make / commands / reserved / seat / seem / take / soon / take / mind

1. You __________ you're having a good evening.
2. I'll be right back to __________ your order.
3. I'll __________ you to the beautiful lakeside seat by the window.
4. Do you have any __________ preference?
5. That table is __________, but here's a nice table for three.
6. I'll call you just as __________ as we are ready.
7. This seat __________ a fine view of the lakeside.
8. If you don't mind waiting, we can ________ a table for you in about 15 minutes.
9. Would you __________ if we sit on that table by the window?

Reading

Read the following story and answer the questions with five minutes.

▪ Seating the Guest

Restaurant receptionists stand at the entrance of the restaurant, dressed up in formal uniforms, waiting to greet the customers. Upon their arrival, the receptionists must quickly check if the customers made a reservation then, if so, check the number reserved guests. After guiding the customers to their allocated table, the staff should offer a sincere and polite statement to enjoy their time. Moreover, they should always greet customers with a cheerful smile, and use polite words and act with a respectful attitude.

These are suggested steps for directing customers: firstly, the waiter/waitress, mindful of the customers, should stay 2-3 steps in front of the customers; secondly, they should be conscious of where their customers are to avoid leaving them behind; thirdly, they should ask if the customers have a desirable seat in mind; fourthly, if a couple arrives, try to help the lady get seated first; lastly, make sure to act in a polite manner when taking the customers' coats or jackets.

Questions For Discussion

1. How should a waiter/waitress guide a customer?
2. What service should the waiter/waitress offer after guiding the customers to a table?
3. What factors must carefully be considered when guiding a customer to a table?

Role Play of Receptionist

1. Do a role play of escorting a guest visiting the restaurant without a reservation.
2. Do a role play of escorting a reserved guest to the table.

Lesson 3 Coffee Shop

Dialogue One

(***W***: *Waiter, Waitress* ***G1***: *Guest 1,* ***G2***: *Guest 2*)

(Taking a beverage order)

W: Good afternoon, ma'am. How are you?

G1: Fine, thank you.

W: Here's your menu, ma'am. What would you like to have, ma'am?

G1: I'm not sure, now. Can you come back in just a minute?

W: Yes. Please take your time, ma'am.

(Later)

Would you like to order now, ma'am?

G1: Yes, please. I'd like Irish coffee, please.

G2: Coffee with cream, please.

W: Thank you, ma'am.

(Later)

Would you like a refill on your coffee, ma'am?

G1: No, thanks. I'm full.

G2: Yes, please. Um. And could I have more water, please?

W: Sure, I'll be right back with that.

Key Points

* Can you come back in just a minute?
  잠시 후에 와 주시겠어요?
* Would you like to order now?
  지금 주문을 받을까요?
* Could I have some more water, please?
  물 좀 더 주시겠어요?

Dialogue Two

(***W***: *Waiter*, *Waitress* ***G***: *Guest*)

(Taking an order for breakfast)

W: Good morning, sir. Here are your menus. What would you like for breakfast?

G: I'll have hash brown potatoes, a corn muffin, ham and eggs.

W: How would you like your eggs, sir?

G: A fried egg and sunny-side-up.

W: Would you like some drinks, sir?

G: Let me have coffee.

W: How would you like your coffee, please?

G: Regular, please.

W: Would you care for anything else, sir?

G: No. That's all.

W: Thank you for your order, sir. I'll get them right away.

(Later)

Would you like some more coffee, sir?

G: Yes, just a little more, please. And can I get more water?

W: Sure, sir.

Key Points

* Here are your menus.
  여기 메뉴가 있습니다.
* How would you like your eggs?
  계란을 어떻게 해드릴까요?
* Would you like some more coffee?
  커피를 좀 더 드시고 싶습니까?

Dialogue Three

(***W***: *Waiter, Waitress* ***G***: *Guest*)

(Taking an order for an American breakfast)

W: Good morning, sir. Are you ready to order now, sir?

G: I haven't seen a menu yet. May I see a menu?

W: I'm sorry, here is the menu, sir.

G: I want to order an American breakfast.

W: What kind of juice would you like, sir?

G: Tomato juice, please.

W: How would you like your eggs, sir?

G: Turn over, please.

W: Which one would you like, sir- bacon, sausage or ham, sir?

G: I'll take bacon. Have it done very crisp, please.

W: Certainly, sir. Is there anything else, sir?

G: Regular coffee, please.

W: Thank you for your order, sir. I'll be right with you.

Key Points

* What kind of juice would you like?
  무슨 종류의 주스를 마시고 싶습니까?
* Have it done very crisp, please.
  파삭파삭하게 해 주십시오.
* I'll be right with you.
  곧바로 가지고 오겠습니다.

Dialogue Four

(***W***: *Waiter, Waitress* ***G***: *Guest*)

(Taking an order for a Continental Breakfast)

W: Good morning, ma'am. May I take your order?

G: Yes. I want to have a continental breakfast.

W: What kind of fruit juice will you have, ma'am?

G: Oh, pineapple juice, please.

W: We have some bread and cornflakes, and oatmeal porridge.

G: I'll have cornflakes with milk and corn muffins with marmalade.

W: Will there be anything else, ma'am?

G: No, That's all.

W: Thank you, ma'am. I'll bring them right away.

(After a while)

Did you enjoy the breakfast, ma'am?

G: Yes, very much!

W: I'm glad you enjoyed it.

Key Points

* May I take your order?

  주문받을까요?

* Did you enjoy the breakfast?

  아침식사가 좋았습니까?

Dialogue Five

(***W***: *Waiter, Waitress* ***G1***: *Guest,* ***G2***: *Guest*)

(Taking an order for lunch)

W: Good afternoon, sir. What would you like to order for lunch?
G1: Well. Beef steak and french fries, please.
W: How would you like your steak, sir?
G1: I'd prefer it medium, please.
W: What kind of dressings would you like, sir?
G1: I'd like French dressing on my salad.
W: Would you like a high chair for your child?
G2: Yes, please.
W: What would you like to have, ma'am?
G2: Hamburger steak, orange juice and some coffee, please.
W: What kind of drinks would you like, sir?
G1: I'd like some French red wine with my meal. What would you recommend?
W: I would recommend the Muscadet. This wine has a full body.
G1: I'd like that one, please.
W: Thank you so much. I'll bring them right away, sir.
(Later)
G1: Waiter! I asked for this to be a medium steak. This isn't medium.
W: I'm very sorry. I'll take it back and have it cooked some more.
G1: Thanks.

Key Points 

* What kind of dressings would you like? 무슨 종류의 드레싱을 좋아 하십니까?
* I'd like some French red wine with my meal.
  식사하는데 프랑스 레드와인을 마시고 싶습니다.
* This wine has a full body. 이 와인은 아주 감칠맛이 있습니다.

Dialogue Six

(***W***: *Waiter, Waitress* ***G1***: *Guest 1,* ***G2***: *Guest 2*)

(Taking an order for dinner)

W: How are you this evening, sir?

G1: I'm just fine. Thank you.

W: I'll show you to your table, sir. This way, please.

G1: It's a nice seat. Thanks.

W: Can I have your order now, sir?

G1: What is today's special menu? Do you recommend it?

W: Today's special is filet mignon, sir. It's very tasty.

G1: Well, I'd like to order two filet mignons.

W: How would you like your steak, sir?

G1: Medium rare, please.

G2: Medium, please.

W: What would you like for soups, sir?

G1: Vegetable soups, please.

W: What kind of salad dressing would you like, sir?

G1: Thousand Island, please.

G2: Italian dressing, please. French dressing

W: Would you care for some wine, sir?

G1: Which wine would go best with filet mignon?

W: I'd suggest a sweet red wine to go with your steak.

W: Could I serve you anything else, sir?

G2: I'll have a coke, please.

W: I'll be back with the drinks.

(Later)

W: Would you care for some dessert, sir?

G1 : What do you have?

W : We have a strawberry ice cream, lemon sorbert, coffee, and peach Melba, sir.

G2 : Peach Melba, please.

W : Thank you, sir. We hope you enjoyed your dinner.
It's one of our chef's specialities.

G1 : It was truly excellent.

W : I'm glad you liked it.

Key Points

* I'd suggest a sweet red wine to go with your steak. 손님의 스테이크 요리에 어울리는 것으로 단맛이 있는 레드와인을 드시는 것이 좋습니다.
* I'll be back with the drinks.
곧 손님이 주문한 메뉴를 제공하겠습니다.
* It's one of our chef's specialities.
그것은 우리 식당의 특별요리 중의 하나입니다.

■ Language Choices 1

1. May I take your order, ma'am?
2. What would you like to order for breakfast?
3. Can I have your order now, sir?
4. Are you ready to order, sir?
5. What would you like to have?
6. Would you like to order now, ma'am?
7. Would you care to order for dinner?
8. What are you going to order, sir?
9. What do you want to order, sir?
10. What would you like for dinner?

■ Language Choices 2

1. How would you like your eggs, ma'am?
2. How do you want your eggs done, sir?

■ Language Choices 3

1. What kind of dressing do you want, sir?
2. Which kind of dressing would you like to have, ma'am?
3. What type of dressing do you want, sir?

■ Language Choices 4

1. What kind of soup do you like, sir?
2. Would you like a soup, ma'am?
3. What kind of soup will you have?
4. What kind of soup do you want, sir?

■ Language Choices 5

1. Would you care for any dessert, sir?
2. What would you like for your dessert, ma'am?
3. What will you have for dessert, ma'am?
4. What would you care to have for your dessert, sir?
5. What kind of dessert will you have, ma'am?

■ Language Choices 6

1. What would you like to drink, sir?
2. Would you care for something to drink, sir?
3. Do you want some more coffee?
4. Anything to drink, sir?
5. Would you like some drinks?
6. What are you going to drink, sir?
7. What kind of juice do you want, ma'am?
8. Can I get you something to drink, sir?
9. What kind of drinks would you like, ma'am?
10. Which do you want to drink, coffee or tea?
11. Which would you prefer, juice or coffee?

Practice 

Step 1. Use the words or phrases in the box to fill in the spaces below.

ready / refill / your eggs / done / prefer / cooked / suggest / order

1. I'll take it back and have it _________ some more.
2. I'd _________ it medium, please.
3. I'd _________ a sweet red wine to go with your steak.
4. How would you like _________?
5. Would you like to _________ now?
6. Are you _________ to order now?
7. Have it _________ very crisp, please.
8. Would you like a _________ on your coffee?

Step 2. Discuss this question with a group of three or four students.

1. My guests are provided with the best service in the world. What does this mean?

Reading

Read the following story and answer the questions with five minutes.

■ Coffee Shop

Coffee shops are generally located where customers can access them conveniently. They serve soft beverages such as coffee and tea, and also provide breakfast and western meals. The prices are comparatively inexpensive and reasonable, and customers are drawn to use them as meeting places. They can also act as Italian or Korean restaurants if none are present in the hotel.

When taking an order, the waiter/waitress needs to actively explain the details of menu selections demonstrating their expertise and skills in the area. The wants and needs of customers must be acknowledged accurately from their perspective. Coffee shops are run all through the day without any breaks, and some places even operate 24 hours a day.

Questions For Discussion

1. What kind of food and beverages do coffee shops generally offer in their menus?
2. What role do hotel coffee shops play for the customers?
3. What generally are the trading hours of a hotel coffee shop?
4. Coffee shops are one of the most popular venues at hotels. Why is this the case?

Role Play of Coffee Shop Waiter(Waitress)

1. Do a role play of the waiter or waitress taking an order for a beverage.
2. Do a role play of the waiter or waitress taking an order for American breakfast or Continental breakfast.
3. Do a role play of the waiter or waitress taking an order for lunch(or dinner).

Lesson 4 French Restaurant Service

- Dialogue One
- Dialogue Two
- Dialogue Three
- Dialogue Four

Dialogue One

(***W***: *Waiter, Waitress* ***G***: *Guest*)

(Recommending a special menu for dinner)

W: Good evening, ma'am. Here's the menu.

G: Do you recommend any special menu today?

W: Yes. We have some fresh sole.
May I suggest filet of sole with Almonds, ma'am?

G: Okay. I'll get that.

W: What would you like with that, ma'am?

G: Baked potato with sour cream, please.

W: What would you like for the soup?

G: Vegetable soup, please.

W: Ma'am, which kind of salad dressing would you prefer - French, Thousand Island, Italian, Russian or oil and vinegar?

G: French dressing, please.

W: Would you like some wine before dinner?

G: White wine, please.

W: Which one would you prefer, dry or sweet?

G: I'd prefer the dry one.

W: Would you like anything else, ma'am?

G: Not at the present moment.

W: Thank you for your order. We'll be ready with your order very soon.
(Later)
Here is your food. Enjoy your dinner.

G : Thank you.

Key Points 

* Do you recommend any special menu today?
  오늘의 특별 메뉴를 추천해 주시겠습니까?
* Would you care for some wine before dinner?
  식사 전에 어떤 와인을 드시겠습니까?
* What kind of salad dressing would you prefer?
  무슨 종류의 드레싱을 좋아하십니까?

Dialogue Two

(***W***: *Waiter, Waitress* ***G***: *Guest*)

(Taking an order for lunch)

W: Good afternoon, sir? May I take your order for lunch?

G: I'll have sirloin steak and a glass of red wine.

W: How would you like your steak cooked, sir?

G: Medium rare, please. What vegetables come with the steak?

W: Baked potatoes and green peas with diced carrots.
What would you like as an appetizer, sir?

G: I would like Smoked Scotch Salmon.

W: What kind of soup do you want, sir?

G: What would you suggest?

W: I recommend the vegetable soup.

G: OK. The vegetable soup, then.

W: Ok, sir. Your order won't take long, sir.
Here's your steak, sir.

G: I dropped my fork on the floor. May I have a new one and a new napkin?

W: Yes, I'll get them for you right away. Please call us if you need further assistance.
We will serve you right away.
(Later)
Are you through, sir?

G: Yes.

W: Shall I take the plates away, sir?

G: Yes, please.

W: What will you have for dessert? We have coffee, mango, ice cream, peach Melba, lemon sorbet.

G: Lemon sorbet, please.

Key Points 

* How would you prefer your steak cooked? 스테이크를 어떻게 해드릴까요?
* What would you like as an appetizer?
애피타이저로 어떤 것을 드시면 좋겠습니까?
* Shall I take the plates away, sir? 접시를 치울까요?

Dialogue Three

(***W***: *Waiter, Waitress* ***G***: *Guest*)

(Taking an order for Table D'hote)

W: What would you like for dinner, sir?
This is the table d'hote and that is a la carte.

G: Let me see. I'd like to choose the a la carte menu.

W: Would you like some appetizer, sir?

G: I'll have a shellfish cocktail, and then French onion soup.

W: May I take an order for your main dish now, sir?

G: Yes, I'll also have prime rib and baked potato with sour cream.

W: Certainly, sir. How would you like your steak, sir?

G: I would like it medium rare, please. How long do you think it will take?

W: About 25 minutes, sir. What kind of salad dressing would you like, sir?

G: Do you have any Blue cheese dressing?

W: I'm afraid we don't have it. I would recommend the French dressing.

G: OK. French dressing, please.

(Later)

W: How was your meal, sir?

G: Very good.

W: Are you done with your meal, sir?

G: Yes, please.

W: Would you like anything for dessert, sir?

G: Yes, I would. What do you have?

W: We have ice cream, orange sherbet, chocolate mousse, blackberry pie and fresh fruits.

G: Give me blackberry pie, please.

W: Thank you very much. I'll get it right away, sir.

Key Points

* Would you like anything to start, sir?
  먼저 어떤 것을 드시겠습니까?
* I would like it medium rare, please.
  중간보다 약간 덜 익혀주십시오.
* Are you done with your meal, sir?
  식사를 마쳤습니까?

Dialogue Four

(***W***: *Waiter, Waitress* ***G***: *Guest*)

(Taking an order for dinner)

W: May I take your order for dinner, sir?

G: What's the special dish you would recommend?

W: The chef's specialties for today are the filet of beef steak with mushroom sauce and the poached salmon with white wine sauce.

G: I'll try the filet of beef steak. What vegetables come with the steak?

W: We have a baked potato, carrots and peas. How would you like your steak, sir?

G: Well-done, please.

W: What kind of soup will you have, sir?

G: What is today's soup?

W: We have French onion and vegetable soup.

G: Vegetable soup, please.

W: What kind of salad dressing would you like, sir? We have Thousand Island, French, Italian and Blue cheese dressing.

G: Thousand Island dressing, please.

W: May I suggest a bottle of house red wine to go with your steak, sir?

G: OK. And which wine would you recommend to me?

W: I want to recommend the Chateau Margaux(Red Bordeaux).

G: Very good. Please give me that one.

W: Yes. I'll be back with your drink in a moment, sir.

(Later)

Dinner is served. Please be careful. The plate is very hot. Enjoy your meal, please.

(Later)

How was everything?

G : Delicious, thanks.

W : Excuse me. May I take your plates, sir?

G : Sure.

Key Points 

* How was everything? 잘 드셨습니까?
* May I take your plates? 접시를 치워드릴까요?
* The chef's specialties for today are the filet of beef steak with mushroom.
  오늘 주방장의 특별 요리는 버섯을 곁들인 필레 스테이크 요리입니다.

■ Language Choices 1

1. Are you finished with your dinner, sir?
2. Are you done with this breakfast?
3. Are you done, sir?
4. Are you through, ma'am?

■ Language Choices 2

1. May I clear the table, sir?
2. May I take it(them), sir?
3. Shall I remove your plate, ma'am?

■ Language Choices 3

1. How was your meal, ma'am?
2. Did you enjoy your meal, sir?
3. Are you enjoying your meal, ma'am?

■ Language Choices 4

1. How do you want your steak, ma'am?
2. How would you like your steak, sir?
3. How would you like your steak done, sir?
4. How would you prefer your steak, sir?

Practice

Step 1. Use the words or phrases in the box to fill in the spaces below.

would / suggest / dropped / go with / think / take / be ready / plates

1. How long do you __________ it will take?
2. What ____________ you suggest for the soup?
3. May I suggest a bottle of house red wine to ____________ your steak?
4. May I ____________ filet of sole with Almonds?
5. Your order won't ____________ long.
6. I ____________ my fork on the floor.
7. We'll ____________ for your order very soon.
8. May I take your ___________?

Step 2. Discuss this question with a group of three or four students.

> The employees at the Jinju Hotel know that their job is to give the best possible service to the guests. The employees are always friendly and courteous to the guests.

1. What does this mean?

Reading

Read the following story and answer the questions with five minutes.

■ French Restaurant Service

French service is French food of superb quality that European nobles used to enjoy. It is mainly served in up-market restaurants where the elegance and glamor of the food can effectively be portrayed. Waiters and waitress play an important role in French restaurants, because they are the frontline employees who serve French food and drinks and carry out customer orders.

Because waiters and waitresses work very closely with the customers, they must concern themselves with excellent outfits, appearance, personal hygiene, service attitude, and polite manners. They also need to be well aware of the menus and hotel facilities to be prepared for any inquiries and provide consumer satisfaction.

When providing French service, firstly, the waiters and waitresses should be experienced and skillful; secondly, service methods should be up to the standards of restaurants that use á la carte menus; thirdly, services should be made with politeness, formality and dignity; and lastly, customers' appetite should be further enhanced by use of presentation.

Questions For Discussion

1. What characteristics must employees possess to work at a French restaurant?
2. What are the unique features of French cuisine?
3. How can waiters and waitresses to provide great French service?

Role Play of French Restaurant's Waiter

1. Do a role play of taking a meal order for special menu from the guest at a French restaurant.
2. Do a role of taking a meal order from the guest at a French restaurant.

Lesson 5 Korean Restaurant Service

Dialogue One

(***W***: *Waiter, Waitress* ***G***: *Guest*)

(Recommending particular Korean dishes)

W: Good evening, sir. May I help you, sir?

G: Yes, please.

W: What would you like to order for dinner?

G: I don't know anything about Korean food. Is there anything particular you would recommend for me?

W: Yes, I would like to suggest the Bulgogi, sir. Bulgogi is one of the most popular Korean dishes among the foreigners in our restaurant.

G: What is it?

W: It's sliced beef that you roast on a charcoal burner right at your table. Bulgogi consists of strips of beef charcoal-roasted over a brazier at the table after it has been marinated in a complex mixture of soy sauce, sesame oil and spices for a few hours. We usually have it with rice and wrap it in raw lettuce.

G: Very good. I've never tried Bulgogi, but I'll have it this time.

W: Would you care for something to drink, sir? We have beer, wine and traditional Korean liquor.

G : What's traditional Korean liquor?

W: It's called 'Soju'. It's one of the most popular drinks among Korean people. I think 'Soju' goes very well with this.

G: Oh, good. I'll try it. Bring a bottle of Soju, please.

W: Thank you. I'll be right out with you to take your order, sir.

Key Points

* Is there anything particular you would recommend for me?
  나를 위해 특별히 추천할만한 것이 있습니까?
* I would like to suggest the Bulgogi.
  불고기를 추천하고 싶습니다.
* Would you care for something to drink?
  어떤 것을 마시고 싶습니까?

Dialogue Two

(***W***: *Waiter, Waitress* ***G***: *Guest*)

(Taking an order for Hanjeongsik)

W: Good afternoon, sir. Can I have your order now, sir?

G: I'm waiting for my company now. If a man asks for Mr. Brown, please direct him to me.

W: Certainly, sir.

(After a while)

Are you ready to order, sir?

G: Yes, please. We're not sure which to order, but we want to have traditional Korean food. Could you help us to order a Korean dish?

W: Yes, sir. I'd like to recommend Hanjeongsik.

Hanjeongsik is one of the typical Korean style dishes. It consists of a bowl of rice and soup with many side dishes. The side dishes consist of bean sprouts, cabbage Kimchi, an assortment of broiled seafood, stewed beef ribs, brochette of broiled beef, deep fried shrimp and vegetables. And a fried or broiled fish is also served. I think you will have a good opportunity to eat the typical Korean food.

G: Very good. We'll have that.

W: Can I get you something to drink, sir?

G: Yes. We want to drink beer. Bring three bottles of beer, please.

(Later)

W: I'm sorry your order was delayed. Here's Hanjeongsik. Enjoy your meal, please.

G: Waitress! We need some salt. There's none on the table.

W: Yes. I'll get it right away, sir.

Key Points 

* Hanjeongsik is one of the typical Korean style dishes.
  한정식은 전형적인 한국 스타일의 식사 중 하나입니다.
* I'm sorry your order was delayed.
  주문한 것이 늦어서 죄송합니다.

Dialogue Three

(***W***: *Waiter, Waitress* ***G***: *Guest*)

(Taking an order for Broiled Beef Ribs Table D'hote)

W: Good evening, sir? How many in your party, sir?

G: Four of us.

W: I'll show you to your table. This way, please. How about this table, sir?

G: Oh! Very good. Thanks.

W: Leave your coat with me, sir. Here's the menu, sir.

(Later)

What would you like to order for dinner?

G: We don't know about Korean food. Is there any particular Korean dish you would recommend?

W: Yes. I can suggest our broiled beef ribs table d'hote.
Many people like it, sir.

G: What is it?

W: It consists of broiled beef ribs, assorted fresh vegetables, seasonal wild greens and spinach, pan-fried fish and vegetables with egg, rice and soup, fresh fruits in season.

G: Is it spicy?

W: No, it isn't.

G: That sounds good. Let us give it a try. We'll have the broiled beef ribs table d'hote.

W: That'll take a while to cook. Would you mind waiting?

G: That's okay.

W: Thanks a lot. We'll try to prepare your order as soon as possible.

Key Points 

* Is there any particular Korean dish you would recommend?
  추천할 수 있는 특별한 한국 음식이 있습니까?
* We'll try to prepare your order as soon as possible.
  가능한 빨리 주문한 것을 제공하겠습니다.

■ Language Choices 1

1. What do you suggest this evening?
2. What would you recommend for lunch?
3. What would you suggest as a main dish?
4. Would you help us to choose Korean food?
5. Can you suggest any Korean dish?
6. Could you recommend anything for my lunch?
7. Is there anything you can recommend?
8. Do you have any particular dish you would recommend this evening?

■ Language Choices 2

1. Would you like to try some traditional Korean dishes?
2. Will you try to have Korean food?

■ Language Choices 3

1. What's your specialty in this restaurant?
2. What is today's special menu?
3. What would you recommend for today's special?
4. What's good on the menu today?
5. Is there a specialty of this restaurant today?
6. Would you recommend any special menu this evening?
7. What do you think I should particularly have this evening?
8. Do you have any special menu for my lunch?
9. Can you suggest a special menu for me?
10. What's good here?
11. May I suggest our specialty today?

■ Language Choices 4

1. Filet mignon is one of the specialties in our restaurant.
2. It's one of the specialties this evening.
3. This is our specialty.
4. This is chef's special menu for lunch.
5. This is chef's special menu for lunch.
6. The chef's specialties for today are filet mignon and lobster.
7. Bulgogi is one of the most popular korean dishes among foreigners in our restaurant.
8. Kalbi-jim(Beef rib stew) is our restaurant's most popular meal.

Practice

Step 1. Use the words or phrases in the box to fill in the spaces below.

help / recommend / have / tried / direct / prepare / something / party

1. Would you care for _________ to drink?
2. We usually _________ it with rice and wrap it in raw lettuce.
3. Could you _________ us to order a Korean dish?
4. We'll try to _________ your order as soon as possible.
5. If a man asks for Mr. Brown, please _________ him to me.
6. I've never _________ Bulgogi, but I'll have it this time.
7. Is there anything particular you would _________ for me?
8. How many in your _________?

Step 2. Discuss in groups why it is important to describe Korean dishes.

Reading

Read the following story and answer the questions with five minutes.

▪ Korean Restaurant Service

Korean restaurants offer traditional Korean food that fully occupies the space on the table.

Traditional Korean cuisine such as bulgogi, sinseollo, kimchi, and hot pots originated from old royal monarchies. However, it is a fact that there have been difficulties in developing diversities in Korean cuisine compared to that of western foods, due to limited contemporary cooking styles.

The serving methods of Korean foods are as follows:

When a customer arrives at the restaurant, the waiter/waitress greets him/her respectfully, confirms their booking status and then guides them to their reserved table.

The waiter/waitress pulls out the chair a little but from behind the customer to help him/her be seated comfortably.

The waiter/waitress shows the customer the menu.

The waiter/waitress also Informs the customer of foods that may take slightly longer to cook.

When serving new dishes, used plates should be taken away.

Questions For Discussion

1. Why has Korean cuisine diversified less than foods in western cuisines?
2. What are the signature dishes of Korean cuisine?
3. How should Korean food be served?

Role Play of Korean Restaurant' s Waitress

1. Do a role play of recommending particular Korean dishes.
2. Do a role play of taking an order for a traditional Korean dish.

Lesson 6 Bar Service

- Dialogue One
- Dialogue Two
- Dialogue Three
- Dialogue Four
- Dialogue Five
- Dialogue Six
- Dialogue Seven

Dialogue One

(***W***: *Waiter, Waitress* ***G1***: *Guest 1,* ***G2***: *Guest 2*)

(Taking a whisky order)

W: Good evening, sir. How many are there in your group?

G1: I need a table for two. Do you have a table with fine view?

W: Sure. This way, please. This seat commands a fine view of the riverside.

G1: Oh! It's very beautiful.

W: Can I get you something to drink, sir?

G1: A Scotch and Soda with ice, please.

W: What brand of Scotch would you like to have, sir?

G1: Johnnie Walker Red, please.

W: What kind of drinks would you like, sir?

G2: I'll have a glass of whisky.

W: What kinds of whisky would you like, sir?

G2: Well. What kinds of whisky have you got?

W: We have Scotch, Irish, American and Canadian whisky.

G2: I'll have an American whiskey.

W: How would you like your whisky, sir?

G2: On the rocks, please. The best you have.

W: Thank you for your order, sir.

Key Points 

* Can I get something to drink? 마실 것 좀 드릴까요?
* What kinds of whisky have you got? 어떤 종류의 위스키가 있습니까?
* How would you care for your whisky? 위스키를 어떻게 드릴까요?
* The best you have. 좋은 것으로 주세요.

Dialogue Two

(***W***: *Waiter, Waitress* ***G1***: *Guest 1,* ***G2***: *Guest 2,* ***G3***: *Guest 3*)

(Taking orders for Brandy and Gin)

W: Good evening, gentlemen. May I help you?

G1: Yes, I'd like a Cognac, please.

W: Which brand would you prefer, sir?

G1: Well. A shot of Remy Martin X.O. No ice, no water, please.

W: If you take a bottle, we can give you 15% discount and serve you complimentary side dishes.

G1: OK. I'll take a bottle. But please keep it here if I don't finish it today.

W: Sure. We'll number your bottle and keep it until you come back next time.

W: What would you like, sir?

G2: Give me a Gilbey's, please.

W: Would you like it straight up or on the rocks?

G2: Straight up, please. And could you give us dry snacks?

W: And you, sir?

G3: Well, I'd like a gin and tonic, regular, please.

W: Thank you, sir.

Key Points 

* Please keep it here if I don't finish it today.
만일 오늘 다 못 마시면 그것을 여기에 보관하여 주십시오.

* Would you like it straight up or on the rocks?
스트레이트 혹은 온 더 락으로 드시겠습니까?

Dialogue Three

(***B***: *Bartender* ***G1***: *Guest 1*, ***G2***: *Guest 2*)

(Taking orders for Rum and Vodka)

B: Good evening, Mr. Brown and Mr. Wilson. Nice to see you again. Please sit at this table.

G1: Nice to see you, too.

B: What would you like to drink this evening, Mr. Brown and Mr. Wilson?

G1: I'll have a Bacardi Light.

B: Which do you prefer straight up or on the rocks, Mr. Brown?

G1: Straight up, please.

B :Would you like to have your usual drink, Mr. Wilson?

G2: Sure, A Smirnoff Black Label.

B: Thank you. I will be back with your order.

(Later)

Here they are. Enjoy your drinks.

(Later)

G1: Give me another, please.

B :Yes, sir. Here you are, Mr. Brown.

Key Points 

* What would you like to drink this evening?

오늘 저녁에는 무엇을 마시고 싶습니까?

* I'll have a Bacardi Light.

바카디 라이트를 마시고 싶습니다.

Dialogue Four

(***W***: *Waiter, Waitress* ***G1***: *Guest 1*, ***G2***: *Guest 2*, ***G3***: *Guest 3*)

(Taking orders for liqueur and beer)

W: Good evening, ladies and gentleman.

G1: Do you have a table available for three?

W: Sure, sir. This way, please. We have a table near the window with a good view.

G1: Non smoking will be better.

W: Here‘s your seat. It's in the non smoking section, sir. How do you like your seat?

G2: Oh, it's a nice one. Thanks.

W: You're welcome. May I help you, ladies and gentleman?

G1: We don't know what we want. Wait a moment, please.

(Later)

I'd like a glass of Drambuie.

G2: A glass of Bailey's Irish cream, please.

W: What would you like, ma'am?

G3: A beer would be fine.

W: Do you want any special brand, ma'am?

G3: No. Anything will be fine. I'm very thirsty.

W: And what kind of side dishes would you like?

G1: I'd like the dry snacks. Can you bring us some peanuts?

W: Yes, I'll bring them right away.

(Later)

Here they are. Taste these liqueurs, please. Would these be all right?

G1: Yes. Very good.

W: Thank you very much.

Key Points 

* It's in the non smoking section. 금연구역입니다.
* Do you want any special brand?
  어떤 특별한 브랜드를 원하십니까?
* I'll bring them right away.
  곧 그것을 갖다드리겠습니다.

Dialogue Five

(***W***: *Waiter, Waitress* ***G1***: *Guest 1*, ***G2***: *Guest 2*, ***G3***: *Guest 3*)

(Taking an order for a Cocktail, case Ⅰ)

W: Good evening, gentlemen. Do you have any seat preference?

G1: Yes, a table for three by the window? Non smoking will be better.

W: Certainly, sir. This way, please. Will this table be all right, sir?

G2: Oh! Yes. It's beautiful.

W: What will you have, sir? Martini is on promotion this week. If you select it, we can give you one complimentary side dish, sir.

G1: OK. I'd like to select a Martini today.

W: How would you like it, sir?

G1: Don't make it strong, please.

G2: A Singapore Sling, please. And make it with a lot of Soda water, please.

W: And what would you like, sir?

G3: I'll drive. I want a cocktail without alcohol.

W: We have Pussy Foot, Fruit Punch, Virgin Mary, Shirley Temple, Virgin Pina Colada and Lemonade. Which would you prefer, sir?

G3: Pussy Foot, please.

W: Thank you, sir. Will you have some side dishes?
We have mixed nuts, fresh fruit and so on.

G1: Give us fresh fruit, please.

W: Yes, I will return with your drinks in a few minutes.

Key Points

* If you select it, we can give you one side dish as a complimentary.
만일 그것을 선택하신다면, 무료로 안주를 드릴 수 있습니다.
* Make it with a lot of Soda water.
그것에 탄산수를 많이 넣어 주십시오.
* Don't make it strong, please.
그것을 너무 진하게 하지 말아 주십시오.

Dialogue Six

(***B***: *Bartender* ***G***: *Guest*)

(Taking an order for a Cocktail, case Ⅱ)

B: Good evening, sir. Here is the cocktail list. What will you have, sir?

G: I'll have a Manhattan, please.

B: Would you like it straight up or on the rocks, sir?

G: On the rocks, please. If I drink from the Mini-bar in my room, I can drink cheaper. But I can't meet the nice friendly faces.

B: We're really happy to see you, sir.

G: You speak English very well.

B: In this line of business, we have to speak English fluently because we talk with many guests.

G: I know it, but that's unusual.

B: Here it is.

(Later)

Can I get you another Manhattan, sir?

G: Sure. I'd like another one.

B: Would you like some pop corn or peanuts?

G: Yes, please.

B: How's your Manhattan?

G: It's really good.

B: That's great.

Key Points 

* Would you like it straight up or on the rocks?
  그것을 스트레이트 혹은 온 더 락으로 하고 싶습니까?
* Can I get you another Manhattan?
  맨하탄 하나 더 주시겠습니까?
* How's your Manhattan?
  맨하탄을 어떻게 해 드릴까요?

Dialogue Seven

(***W***: *Waiter* ***G1***: *Guest 1*, ***G2***: *Guest 2*)

(Taking an order for wine)

W: Good evening, sir. Would you like something to drink?

G1: Yes, I'd like to have a French red wine.

W: Here is our wine list. I'll be back shortly, sir. What brand would you prefer, sir?

G1: Well. I'd like a bottle of Chateau Margaux, Margaux1988(Red Bordeaux). This wine is my favorite one.

W: Which one would you like better, dry or sweet?

G1: Dry, please.

W: What would you have, ma'am?

G2: Can you recommend a white wine?

W: Yes. I'd like to recommend the Chablis, ma'am. This is a full tender wine. And it's very popular with our foreign guests.

G2: OK. I'll try it.

W: Thank you, ma'am. Would you like anything else, ma'am?

G2: Give us some cheese, please.

W: Yes, ma'am.

(Later)

G1: Excuse me, please give us another bottle of wine. And more cheese, please.

W: Sure. Wait a moment.

Key Points

* What brand would you prefer?
  무슨 브랜드를 좋아하십니까?
* It's very popular with our foreign guests.
  외국 손님들이 매우 좋아합니다.

■ Language Choices 1

1. What kind of whisky will you have, sir?
2. What kind of whisky would you like to drink, sir?
3. What brand would you prefer, ma'am?
4. Which brand of scotch would you like, sir?

■ Language Choices 2

1. How would you like your scotch, sir?
2. How would you care for your whisky, sir?

■ Language Choices 3

1. Don't make it strong, please.
2. Make it with soda water, please.
3. I want that without alcohol.
4. Make it with no ice, please.
5. Make that with gin, please.
6. Make this a little sweeter, please.

Practice

Step 1. Use the words or phrases in the box to fill in the spaces below.

brand / keep / commands / popular / mixed / give / serve / drink

1. It's very ________ with our foreign guests.
2. We'll number your bottle and ________ it until you come back next time.
3. Can I get something to ________?
4. If you take a bottle, we can give you 15% discount and ________ you complimentary side dishes.
5. Do you want any special ________?
6. We have ________ nuts, fresh fruit and so on.
7. This seat ________ a fine view of the riverside.
8. Please ________ us another bottle of wine.

Step 2. Look at Dialogue Three again in pairs. Discuss why it is good to try and remember guests?

Step 3. Look at Dialogue Six again. Can you think of more reasons why speaking English is important? Discuss with your parter or group.

Reading

Read the following story and answer the questions with five minutes.

■ Bar Service

Bars provide customers with various types of cocktails and other drinks. Bartenders should always keep their appearance clean and tidy and greet customers with a bright smile. Bartenders should have extensive knowledge and skills over a wide range of beverages so as to ensure they can fulfill the orders of every customer. They should try to remember preferences and unique characteristics of loyal customers who visit frequently. While conversing with customers, the topic should be one that is about the customer's interests. Bartenders should respond politely and keep the customer intrigued. Unlike non-alcoholic beverages, alcoholic beverages can result in binge drinking. Therefore, bartenders should know if a customer has had too much to drink and be equipped to deal with the situation. Accordingly, bartenders should not offer excessive drinks to customers.

Questions For Discussion

1. What kind of knowledge and skills do bartenders need to have?
2. What things must bartenders consider when conversing with a customer?
3. What signs should bartenders monitor when serving customers alcoholic drinks?

Role Play of Bartender(Waiter, Waitress)

1. Do a role play of the waiter or waitress(bartender) taking orders for whisky, Brandy, and Gin in the main bar.
2. Do a role play of the waiter or waitress(bartender) taking orders for Rum, Vodka, liqueur and beer in the main bar.
3. Do a role play of the waiter or waitress(bartender) taking an order for a Cocktail in the main bar.

Restaurant Cashier Service

- Dialogue One
- Dialogue Two
- Dialogue Three
- Dialogue Four

Dialogue One

(***C*** : *Cashier* ***G*** : *Guest*)

(Asking to pay in cash)

C : Did you enjoy your meal, sir?

G : That was excellent.

C : I'm glad to hear that.

G : I'd like to settle my bill now. How much is it?

C : Wait a minute, please. It'll be 97,000 won altogether, sir.

G : What's this total for?

C : Your bill includes a 10% tax and a 10% service charge.
How would you like to pay, sir?

G : In cash. Here's 100,000 won.

C : Thank you, sir. I've 100,000 won. Your change is 3,000 won and here is your receipt.

G : You can keep the change.

C : I'm sorry, sir. No tipping is our policy. Have a nice day.

Key Points

* I'd like to settle my bill now.
  지금 계산하고 싶습니다.
* Your bill includes a 10% tax and a 10% service charge.
  계산서에는 10% 세금과 10%의 서비스료가 포함되어 있습니다.
* How would you like to pay?
  어떻게 지불하시겠습니까?

Dialogue Two

(***C***: *Cashier* ***G***: *Guest*)

(Asking to pay by credit card)

C: How was your lunch, ma'am?

G: It was very delicious. I'd like to pay my bill.

C: The charge for your lunch is 40 dollars, ma'am.

G: Is the service charge included?

C: Yes, a service charge is included in the bill.

G: Do you accept an American Express card?

C: Yes, ma'am. We accept most credit cards except cash card.
May I have your card, please?

G: Here it is.

C: Here's the total amount, ma'am. Could you sign here?

G: All right. Here you are.

C: Here's your receipt and card, ma'am.

G: Thank you.

C: It's been our pleasure serving you. Hope to see you soon, ma'am.

Key Points

* The charge for your lunch is 40 dollars.
  점심값은 40달러입니다.
* It's been our pleasure serving you.
  손님을 모시게 되어 대단히 좋습니다.
* We accept most of credit cards except cash card.
  현금카드를 제외한 대다수의 신용카드들은 받습니다.

Dialogue Three

(***C*** : *Cashier* ***G*** : *Guest*)

(Asking to pay by traveler's Check)

C : Good evening, sir. I hope you enjoyed staying with us.

G : Oh, yes. We enjoyed it very much. I'd like to pay my bill.

C : The full amount is 108,000 won including the tax and service charge.
Shall I make separate bills?

G : No, altogether on one bill and give it to me. I'll pay with traveler's checks.
Do you accept traveler's checks here?

C : Certainly, sir. The total will be ninety-six dollars.

G : Here's one hundred dollar traveler's check.

C : May I have your passport, sir?

G : Here you are. What's the rate of exchange today?

C : It's 1,150 won per dollar today. Sign here with this pen, please.

G : Sure. Here you are.

C : Thank you very much. Here's your change and passport.
I hope I have a chance to serve you again, sir.

Key Points

* I hope you enjoyed staying with us.
즐거운 시간을 가지셨길 바랍니다.
* Shall I make separate bills?
영수증을 분리할 수 있을까요?
* What's the rate of exchange today?
오늘의 환율은 어떻습니까?

Dialogue Four

(***C*** : *Cashier* ***G*** : *Guest*)

(Asking to add the breakfast bill to the room account)

C : Good morning, sir. How was your breakfast?

G : I enjoyed my breakfast very much.

C : Thanks, sir.

G : I'd like to settle my bill.

C : Your bill comes to 40,000 won, sir.

G : Does the bill include the service charge?

C : Yes, it does. Your bill includes the tax and service charge.

G : Ah! I'd like to charge it to my room account.

C : What room are you in?

G : My room is 903. I'll stay there till tomorrow.

C : Excuse me, may I ask your name, sir?

G : Frank Lewis.

C : Wait a moment, sir. The amount will be added to your final room bill, sir. Could you please sign here, sir?

G : Certainly, here it is.

C : Thank you, sir. We hope to serve you again.

Key Points 

* Your bill comes to 40,000 won. 4만원입니다.
* Your bill includes the tax and service charge. 세금과 봉사료가 포함 되었습니다.
* The amount will be added to your final room bill.
  총 합계는 객실료가 가산됩니다.

Dialogue Five

(**C** : *Cashier* **G** : *Guest*)

(Dealing with a miscalculation)

C : Good evening, sir. Can I help you?

G : May I have the bill, please? How much is it?

C : Your bill comes to 55,000 Won, sir.

G : Excuse me. I don't think this is correct.

C : What is it, sir?

G : I'm afraid you've overcharged me. You've charged me for two cocktails, but I only had one. And I never had an other side dish. Look at this.

C : Oh, is that so? I think we made a mistake in your bill.
I'll check it with the bartender right away.
(After a while)
I'm really sorry, sir. You're right. I'll adjust your bill immediately, sir.

G : That's okay. I am very impressed because you've adjusted my bill right away.

C : Thank you, sir. I look forward to serving you again, sir.

Key Points

* I am very impressed. 나는 감동했습니다.
* You made this bill as I had something.
  내가 마신 것을 계산했습니다.
* I think we made a mistake in your bill.
  영수증에 실수가 있었다고 생각합니다.

■ Language Choices 1

1. What's this total for?
2. What's this amount for?
3. What's this for?
4. What's this charge for?
5. What's this item on the bill?

■ Language Choices 2

1. Your bill includes a 10% tax and a 10% service charge, sir.
2. The bill doesn't include a 10% tax and a 10% service charge, sir.
3. A 10% service charge is added to your bill, sir.
4. Is service charge included on this bill.

■ Language Choices 3

1. Do you accept traveler's checks?
2. Can I use the credit card?
3. Can I pay it with this credit card here?
4. Do you take traveler's checks here?

■ Language Choices 4

1. Here's your change and receipt, sir.
2. Here's your receipt and card, ma'am.
3. Here's your change and passport, sir.

Practice

Step 1. Use the words or phrases in the box to fill in the spaces below.

check / settle / serving / accept / give / added / impressed / included / receipt

1. I'll ________ it with the bartender right away.
2. I am very ________ because you adjust my bill right away.
3. We ________ most of credit cards except cash card.
4. Altogether on one bill and ________ it to me.
5. I'd like to ________ my bill now.
6. A service charge is ________ in the bill.
7. It's been our pleasure ________ you.
8. The amount will be ________ to your final room bill.
9. Your change is 3,000 won and here is your ________.

Step 2. Discuss with your partner.

Everyone sometimes makes a mistake. What should you do when you have made a mistake?

1. Ignore it and hope the customer doesn't notice, or tell the customer and apologize. Why?

Reading

Read the following story and answer the questions with five minutes.

■ Restaurant Cashier Service

After finishing their meals, customers head over to the cashier to pay their bills. At this stage, customers can feel very frustrated if forced to wait long or treated unpleasantly, and the perceived service quality of the restaurant can plummet. Cashiers should carry out the calculations quickly, clearly, and accurately, and must make sure to express their sincere gratitude to the customers. They must show polite manners as customers pay, and they must not discriminate customers based on age, appearance, or etiquette.

During conversations, they should enunciate clearly and lower their volume. Even for small issues, cashiers must be patient and make efforts to explain the issue to the customer until he/she understands. Therefore cashiers should express their sincere gratitude when welcoming or giving farewell to customers.

Questions For Discussion

1. How should cashiers act when customers pay to display good service?
2. What points should cashiers consider carefully when customers are paying their bills?
3. What is the most important task for a cashier?

Role Play of Restaurant Cashier

1. Do a role play of the cashier having the guest pay in cash, by credit card and traveler's check.
2. Do a role play of the cashier being asked to add the meal cost to the room account.

Lesson 8 Room Service

- Dialogue One
- Dialogue Two
- Dialogue Three
- Dialogue Four

Dialogue One

(***W***: *Waiter* ***G***: *Guest*)

(Taking an order for breakfast)

W: Good morning. Room service, this is Kim speaking. Can I help you, sir?

G: Sure. I want to have an American breakfast in my room.

W: For how many guests, sir?

G: Just one, please.

W: May I take your order, sir?

G: Sure. I'd like two eggs, toast juice, a grilled sausage, and coffee.

W: How would you like your eggs, sir?

G: I would like to have them scrambled, please.

W: May I have your name and the room number, sir?

G: This is Frank Lewis in room 1107.

W: Would you care for coffee or tea, sir?

G: Bring me coffee, please. How long will it take?

W: It'll take about 20 minutes, but we'll serve your breakfast as soon as possible.

G: Okay. I have an appointment with my friend. I don't have much time.

W: Yes. Thank you for your order, Mr. Lewis.

Key Points 

* How many guests do you want? 몇 명의 것을 원하십니까?
* How long will it take? 얼마나 오래 걸립니까?
* It'll take about 20 minutes, but we'll serve your breakfast as soon as possible. 약 20분 정도입니다만, 가능한 빨리 식사를 제공하겠습니다.

Dialogue Two

(***W***: *Waiter* ***G***: *Guest*)

(Taking an order for a beverage)

W: Good afternoon, room service.
What can I help you with, sir?

G: I'd like to order some beverages in my room.

W: Sure, sir. Would you like to order now, sir?

G: Yes, I'd like to have a cup of coffee and some juice.

W: What kind of coffee and juice do you want, sir?

G: Irish coffee and tomato juice, please.

W: What's your room number, sir?

G: Room 615.

W: Shall I serve you today's newspaper, sir?

G: Yes, please. It's very kind of you.

W: Is there anything else, sir?

G: No. That's all.

W: Your order should take about 15 minutes. I'll have ready as soon as possible.
Thank you for your order, sir.

Key Points 

* Your order should take about 15 minutes.
손님의 주문은 약 15분 걸립니다.
* I'll have ready as soon as possible.
가능한 빨리 갖다 드리겠습니다.
* Shall I serve you today's newspaper?
오늘 신문을 볼 수 있습니까?

Dialogue Three

(***W***: *Waiter* ***G***: *Guest*)

(Taking an order for dinner)

W: Room service speaking. Can I help you, sir?

G: Yes, this is Bill Jones in room 1023. I would like to order for dinner, but I can't find the room service menu.

W: There is a room service menu on the table in your room.

G: Oh, I see. I found it. I'd like to have filet mignon steak, wine and ice cream.

W: How would you prefer your steak, Mr. Jones?

G: Medium rare, please.

W: Which wine would you like to drink, Mr. Jones?

G: A French red wine.

W: Would you like a dry or sweet wine?

G: Sweet, please.

W: What kind of soup do you like, Mr. Jones? We have onion, cream, consomme' with mushroom and mixed vegetable soup.

G: Mixed vegetable soup, please.

W: Anything else, Mr. Jones?

G: No. Thanks.

W: If there is anything else you need, please let me know right away.

G: Sure. I want to have my dinner at seven o'clock. I'd like to have it very hot. Please give me the dinner really hot.

W: We pride ourselves on bringing hot food and drinks. Our waiter will bring it to your room on time. Have a good time, Mr. Jones.

Key Points 

* Medium rare, please. 미디움 레어로 주십시오.
* There is a room service menu on the table in your room.
  객실 테이블 위에 룸서비스 메뉴판이 있습니다.
* If there is anything else you need, please let me know right away.
  만일 필요한 것이 있다면, 곧 바로 알려주십시오.

Dialogue Four

(***W***: *Waiter* ***G***: *Guest*)

(Taking a request for room service delivery)

W: Room Service, may I help you?

G: Sure. I'd like to order my breakfast.

W: Certainly, sir. What would you like, sir?

G: Two eggs, some bread and coffee, please. How long will it take?

W: It'll take about 15 minutes. Is there anything else, sir?

G: No. That's all.

(Later)

G: Who is it?

W: It's room service. May I come in?

G: Come in, please.

W: Good morning, Mr. Brown. I've brought your breakfast. Where shall I put it?

G: Please put it on the table by the window.

W: Shall I pour the coffee now, Mr. Brown?

G: Yes, please. Will you charge it to the room?

W: Certainly, sir. Please call room service anytime if you need anything else. We're always ready for you.

G: Oh, yes.

W: Would you please sign here, Mr. Brown?

G: Sure. Here it is.

W: Thank you very much. Please enjoy your breakfast, Mr. Brown.

Key Points

* I've brought your breakfast.
  아침식사를 가져왔습니다.
* Please call room service anytime if you need anything else.
  만일 다른 것이 필요하시다면 항상 룸서비스로 전화하여 주십시오.

■ Language Choices 1

1. I've brought your meal you ordered, sir.
2. I've brought up dinner from room service, sir.

■ Language Choices 2

1. Please put the wine on the table.
2. Please put it over there by the window.
3. I'll put your meal on the table.

■ Language Choices 3

1. Shall I pour you coffee now, sir?
2. Would you like me to pour you a cup of coffee now?
3. I'll pour it myself.

■ Language Choices 4

1. Please call room service anytime if you need anything else.
2. Please call us when you need something.

■ Language Choices 5

1. We're always ready for you, sir.
2. We're always at your service, ma'am.

Practice

Step 1. Use the words or phrases in the box to fill in the spaces below.

newspaper / guests / like to / order / know / brought / kind / serve / charge

1. I'd like to _________ some beverage in my room.
2. Will you _________ it to the room?
3. I would _________ have them scrambled, please.
4. It'll take about 20 minutes, but we'll _________ your breakfast as soon as possible.
5. It's very _________ of you.
6. If there is anything else you need, please let me _________ right away.
7. Shall I serve you today's _________?
8. I've _________ your breakfast.
9. How many _________ do you want?

Step 2. Read dialogue Four again. Discuss the following in your group.

1. Did the waiter provide good service? Why? Give examples.
2. How do you say goodbye to a guest when you have finished serving him/her? Look again at the dialogues. Think of three other ways to finish your conversation with a guest.

   Ex) I hope you enjoy your stay.

Reading

Read the following story and answer the questions with five minutes.

■ Room Service

The food is hand delivered to guest rooms when room service is ordered. Room service orders are often taken by an order taker over the telephone. Because communication happens over the phone, it is even more important that there be clear understanding between the customer and the order taker. The fundamental politeness and etiquette of room service begin with courteous phone communications.

Room service is defined as delivering food and beverages to guest rooms. When entering a guest room with room service, the waiter/waitress should have a pleasant facial expression. He/she must always respect the privacy of the guest and must never look around the room or ask any questions. He/she must also be accurate in receiving payment and signature from the guest. Room service must be made convenient for delivery 24 hours every day.

Questions For Discussion

1. What is the service method of room service?
2. Through what methods of communication is room service made?
3. What does a waiter/waitress need to be aware of when entering the room?

Role Play of Room Service's Waiter

1. Do a role play of the order taker when ordering food and beverage.
2. Do a role play of the water making a delivery to the room.

Lesson 9 Banquet Service

Dialogue One

(***M*** : *Manager* ***G*** : *Guest*)

(Asking to reserve a Banquet Room)

M : Good afternoon. Banquet Manager. May I help you, sir?

G : Yes, please. This is Mr. Kim from Samsung company. We need a reception for a dinner we're planning. Could you provide me with some information about your facilities for reception?

M : Yes, when is the reception planned for?

G : October 15th.

M : For what time would that be?

G : 6:00 p.m.

M : How many people will be coming?

G : We're planning to have a reception for about 50 people.

M : We have two suitable banquet rooms to use for 50 people at your reception on that date and hour. What sort of service would you like?

G : It'll be a dinner party for our personnel.

M : How much per person do you expect to spend?

G : We're planning about 80,000 won.

M : What kind of food would you like to have?

G : We'll have steak. Will you make up an estimate for this reception including food and beverage? And send me by fax right now.

M : Yes, I'll do so. What's your fax number and telephone number, Mr. Kim?

G : Our fax number is 792～1123 and our telephone number is 792～1124.

M : Thank you. I'll send it right away.

Key Points 

* When is the reception planned for? 언제 리셉션이 있습니까?
* How many people will be coming? 몇 명이 참가합니까?
* How much per person do you expect to spend?
  한 명당 소요예산은 얼마입니까?

Dialogue Two

(***M***: *Manager* ***G***: *Guest*)

(Asking to pre-check the Banquet Room)

B: Good morning, sir. This is the banquet manager, Miss. Kim. How I help you?

G: We're planning to have a seminar on June 11th, at 2 o'clock. I'd like to see the place first. Can I see the banquet room today?

B: Sure. What time will you get here, sir?

G: How about one o'clock this afternoon? Is that all right?

B: Certainly, sir. How many people would there be?

G: Maybe around 300 people. We'll hold the seminar to invite some professors.
(Later)
I called your office this morning. I'd like to see the banquet room first.

B: Yes, sir. We have a good room available for 300 people.
It will be the Sejong Hall. It's on the second floor. This way, please.

G: Oh, it looks good for our seminar. We'd like to have dinner at that time. Will you make up an estimate for our seminar?

B: Certainly, sir. I'll call you at your office when I am ready for you. And if you decide to open your seminar at our hotel, please let me know.

G: Sure. Thank you very much.

Key Points 

* We have a good room available for 300 people.
  300명이 이용할 수 있는 룸이 있습니까?
* It looks good for our seminar. 세미나를 하기에 좋아 보입니다.
* Will you make up an estimate for our seminar?
  세미나를 위해 견적서를 작성하여 주시겠습니까?

Dialogue Three

(***M*** : *Manager*　　***G*** : *Guest*)

(Cancelling a reservation of facilities)

M : Good afternoon, Can I help you, sir?

G : Yes. I'd like to speak to the manager.

M : I'm sorry, sir. He isn't in the office. May I take a message?

G : Yes. I reserved a function room for a family party tomorrow evening, but I'll have to cancel it.

M: May I ask your name, please?

G : Frank Lewis.

M : Okay, Mr. Lewis. I'll make sure the manager will get the message. Thank you for your calling, Mr. Lewis.

Key Points 

* May I take a message? 메시지를 남기겠습니까?
* I'll make sure the manager will get the message.
  지배인이 메시지를 받을 것이라고 확신합니다.

■ Language Choices 1

1. How many people would there be, sir?
2. How many guests are you expecting?

■ Language Choices 2

1. How much are you going to spend per guest
2. How much per person do you expect to spend?

Practice

Step 1. Use the words or phrases in the box to fill in the spaces below.

be / reception / invite / available / food / make sure / people / reserved

1. We'll hold the seminar to ________ some professors.
2. What kind of ________ would you like to have?
3. It'll ________ a dinner party for our personnel.
4. I'll ________ the manager will get the message.
5. How many ________ will be coming?
6. We have a good room ________ for 300 people.
7. We need a ________ for a dinner we're planning.
8. I ________ a function room for a family party tomorrow evening, but I'll have to cancel it.

Step 2. Discuss with your group or partner.

1. When arranging a banquet estimate, what information do you need from the customer? Make a list of at least 4 items.
2. What information do you think the customer will need from you? Make a list.

Reading

Read the following story and answer the questions with five minutes.

■ Banquet Service

Hotel banquets are the main source of revenue for hotels as they have the greatest space and food and beverages for any single operation. In addition, unlike normal restaurants, there are no tables and chairs set up. This is to allow versatility in setup, adapting to the needs and wants of the customer in contents of the event, the number of people, and amount of food and beverages. Banquet rooms are often used for conferences, seminars, birthday parties and weddings.

Questions For Discussion

1. What are the differences between a banquet service and a regular restaurant service?
2. What types of events are mainly held in a banquet room?

Role Play of Banquet's Waiter

1. Do a role play of taking a reservation on a banquet room.
2. Do a role play of pre-checking the banquet room before the event.

Handling Problems

Lesson 1 Room Division Complaints

Introduction

Customers today are generally well-educated, more demanding and sophisticated than ever before. Service failures are commonplace, despite attempts to deliver high quality service. The problem solving abilities of a hotel employee can be evaluated through their management of customer complaints.

The desirable solution for a hotel would be to handle the complaint of a customer before the spread of any negative word-of-mouth. However, if a customer complaint occurs at a restaurant, they must make significant efforts to recover from their service failures.

Dialogue One

(***C***: *Front Clerk* ***G***: *Guest*)

(Dealing with complaints about loud noise in the next room)

C: Good morning, Mr. Lewis. How can I help you?

G: I couldn't sleep all right. I put a "Do not Disturb!" sign on my door, but the people next door kept making noises.

C: Sorry for the inconvenience, Mr. Lewis. We were not reported of this problem.

G: I am checking out right now.

C: I do offer you my sincerest apologies, Mr. Lewis. I'll report our manager about it. I assure you it won't happen again. Please accept our deepest apology, Mr. Lewis. May I give you another room?

G: If you give me another room, I will accept the apology.

C: We'll do our best, Mr. Lewis. Please let us know if there is any further disturbance.

G: I'll do that.

C: Thank you for accepting our apologies, Mr. Lewis.

Key Points 

* I do offer you my sincerest apologies. 진심으로 사과를 드립니다.
* Please let us know if there is any further disturbance.
  만일 더 이상 방해받는다면 저희들에게 알려주십시오.
* Thank you for accepting our apologies. 사과를 받아주셔서 감사합니다.

Dialogue Two

(***C*** : *20 Front Clerk* ***G*** : *Guest*)

(Dealing with complaints about room cleaning)

C : Good morning, Mr. Brown. Can I help you?

G : Good morning.
I'm in room 708 and it's disgusting. I'm extremely annoyed.

C : Oh, dear. Please let me know the details of the problem.

G : My room was just a mess. It's absolutely filthy. It's quite obvious that the room maid hasn't changed the sheets for days. I was really disappointed in your hotel.

C : I'm terribly sorry about that, Mr. Brown. Thanks for the notice. Well, that's strange. The room maid should have cleaned it yesterday and this morning.

G : I know dirt when I see it. The sheets haven't been changed.

C : Ah, I'm sorry to hear that, Mr. Brown. I'll report it to the housekeeping department manager immediately. I apologize to once again. I'll send the room maid up with some clean sheets, and the manager will make sure the room is cleaned. Could you please tell us if you have any more problems?

G : Okay, I'll accept your apology.

C : Thank you for accepting our apologies.

Key Points

* Please let me know the details of the problem.
  불편하게 한 점에 대해 자세히 알려주십시오.
* I'll accept your apology.
  손님의 말씀을 받아들이겠습니다.

■ Language Choices 1

1. Thank you for bringing the matter to my attention.
2. Thank you for bringing your complaints to our attention.

■ Language Choices 2

1. I'm terribly sorry for our mistake.
2. I'm awfully sorry to hear that, ma'am.
3. We're very sorry for the delay, ma'am.
4. I'm most sorry to have kept you waiting, sir.

■ Language Choices 3

1. I do offer you my most sincere apologies, sir.
2. Please accept our deepest apologies, ma'am.

■ Language Choices 4

1. Please let us know if there is any further disturbance.
2. Could you please tell us if you have any problem again?
3. Please don't hesitate to call us if you have any complaints.
4. Please let us know immediately if you have any further concerns.

Practice

Step 1. Use the words or phrases in the box to fill in the spaces below.

inconvenience / apology / accept / report / disgusting / disappointed / changed / cleaned

1. I was really __________ in your hotel.
2. If you give me another room, I will _________ the apology.
3. Please accept our deepest _________.
4. I'm in room 708 and it's _________.
5. The sheets haven't been _________.
6. The room maid should have _________ it yesterday and this morning.
7. Sorry for the _______________.
8. I'll _________ our manager about it.

Step 2. Discuss with you group and make a list.

1. What other complaints could guests have at a hotel? List at least 3 complaints.
2. Read the dialogues again. What are at least three different ways we can apologize to a guest?
3. How would you deal with an angry customer? Should you smile?

Reading

Read the following story and answer the questions with five minutes.

▪ Room Division Complaints

The recovery from service failures can significantly influence the success of a hotel business. When faced with customer complaints, it should be looked at as a great opportunity to improve the hotel's service quality. They should approach the task positively, understand the problem from the perspective of the customer, pinpoint the issue, and then provide the best solution possible. Thus, if the complaint is resolved successfully and the customer is put at ease, it is more likely to increase the credibility of the hotel and increase guest intentions of revisiting the hotel.

Questions For Discussion 

1. The success or failure of a hotel depends on their complaint handling system. Why do you think handling complaints is so crucial?
2. With what attitude must a hotel approach a complaining customer?

Role Play of Front Clerk and Housekeeper for Handling a Complaint. 

1. Do a role play of dealing with complaints made to room department.

☆ Ideas for the guest

- You want more towels.
- Your room is dirty.
- You want extra blankets.

Lesson 2 Restaurant Complaints

- Dialogue One
- Dialogue Two

Dialogue One

(***W***: *Waiter, Waitress* ***G***: *Guest*)

(Dealing with complaints about the food)

G: Excuse me. I'm not happy with this steak.

W: Is there something wrong with your steak?

G: I ordered it well-done, it's completely medium rare. This beef steak is under done. The sight of that blood has made me sick. I can't eat any more.

W: I'm really sorry, sir. There must be some mistake. I'll change it for you right away.

G: No. That's OK. Please cook it a little more. I don't have much time to catch a train. Please hurry up.

W: Yes, sir. Your steak will be here in a minute. Shall I offer a salad while you're waiting?

G: Yes, please.

(After a while)

W: Here's your steak, sir. I hope this is better. How's your steak this time?

G: That's fine.

W: Thank you very much. Again, I'm really sorry today, sir. We'll try to provide you with a better service in the future, sir.

Key Points 

* Is there something wrong with your steak?
  손님의 스테이크에 어떤 잘못된 것이 있습니까?
* I'll change it for you right away. 곧바로 그것을 바꾸어 드리겠습니다.
* How's your steak this time? 이번에 어떻게 스테이크 해 드릴까요?

Dialogue Two

(***W***: *Waiter, Waitress* ***G***: *Guest*)

(Dealing with complaints about unsatisfactory food)

W: Is everything all right, ma'am?

G: Uh-huh, not so good.

W: Is there anything wrong with your sole?

G: I wanted to have some fresh fish, but this isn't.

W: I'm awfully sorry, ma'am. We can serve you another fresh fish again, if you want it.

G: Thanks.

W: I'll change it for you immediately, ma'am.
Um. I'd like to serve you what our chef can suggest.
Just a moment, please.

G: It's so kind of you to do this.

W: The chef suggested 'a fresh salmon steak'. Would you like it, ma'am?

G: Okay. I'll try it.

W: I'll bring your dish immediately. Please don't hesitate to let us know if you have any complaints.

Key Points

* We can serve you another fresh fish again, if you want it.
  만일 원하신다면, 새로운 생선요리를 제공할 수 있습니다.
* Please don't hesitate to let us know if you have any complaints.
  만일 불충분한 것이 있으시면, 저희들에게 알려주시는 것을 망설이지 마십시오.

■ Language Choices 1

1. Please tell us what happened, sir.
2. Please tell us what displeased you, ma'am.
3. What's happened to your room, ma'am?
4. What's taking so long?
5. Is there something wrong with your meal?
6. How much longer do I have to wait for dinner?
7. May I ask what's the problem?

■ Language Choices 2

1. We assure you of perfect service, sir.
2. We'll certainly take steps to see that it won't happen again, sir.

Practice

Step 1. Use the words or phrases in the box to fill in the spaces below.

cook / happy / medium rare / provide / immediately / suggest / change

1. I'll change it for you __________.
2. I ordered it well-done, it's completely __________.
3. I'd like to serve you what our chef can __________.
4. I'll __________ it for you right away.
5. Please __________ it a little more.
6. I'm not __________ with this steak.
7. We'll try to __________ you with a better service in the future.

Step 2. Discuss with your group or partner.

1. Apologizing and proposing action or a solution always calms a guest when there is a complaint. Why?
2. Think of a time when you had a complaint about service. What did you do? How did you feel? What happened?
3. Why is it important to check you customer's order in the restaurant?

Reading

Read the following story and answer the questions with five minutes.

▪ Restaurant Complaints

Evaluation of services is mostly personal opinion of customers, and so every small detail is significant and should be considered. In general, customers complain about these services in restaurants: firstly, they complain when an abnormal substance is found in a customer's meal; secondly, when the taste of their food is peculiar or poor; thirdly, when the meal served is different from the one ordered or it is not served at all; fourthly, if there are heavy delays in serving; and lastly, if the customer's body or clothes are damaged because of faulty equipment or facilities.

In order to resolve customer complaints, these steps should be followed: firstly, the restaurant must listen carefully to the customer complaints; secondly, the reasons or causes of the complaint need to be identified through thorough investigation; thirdly, the appropriate solution should be worked out as soon as possible; fourthly, the resolution method should be proposed to the customer; and lastly, the final results should be monitored as although the complaint has been handled, the reaction of the customer can vary.

Questions For Discussion

1. What are the main causes of restaurant complaints?
2. Describe how a restaurant can handle and resolve customer complaints.

Role Play of Waiter(Waitress) for Handling Complaints

1. Do a role play of dealing with complaints in the restaurant.

☆ Ideas for the guest

- The soup is cold and you have the wrong salad dressing.
- The beer is warm.
- Your order is taking too long.

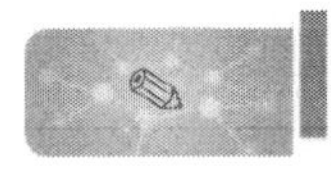

참고문헌

김귀원, HOTEL SERVICE ENGLISH, 백산출판사, 2010.
김동승 외 2명, 호텔특수영어, 백산출판사, 2003.
김영우, English for Hotelier, 2004.
권태영, Talk Talk Hotel English, 기문사, 2007.
김일홍 외 3명, 고급레스토랑실무영어, 백산출판사, 2009.
Kim Hyon-sue 외 3명, Essential English, Brain House, 2003.
배상정, 관광·호텔·항공 실무영어, 기문사, 2011.
임영숙 · 강영욱, 레스토랑 실무영어, 기문사, 2011.

■ 저자소개

하종명

경남대학교 대학원 경영학과 수료(경영학 박사)
경희대학교 경영대학원 관광경영학과(경영학 석사)
한국관광식음료학회 회장, 대한관광경영학회 부회장, 한국관광학회 이사, 관광경영학회 이사,
한국관광평가연구원 책임연구위원, 한국식음료경연대회 조직위원장
현재: 한국국제대학교 호텔관광학과 교수
중국 Hebei College 명예교수, 몽골 Monos University 명예교수

〈저서 및 논문〉
서비스산업론(백산출판사)
항공여행영어회화(백산출판사)
호텔식음료경영 실무(대왕사)
관광호텔 노사관계의 안정성과 영향요인에 관한 실증적 연구 외 다수

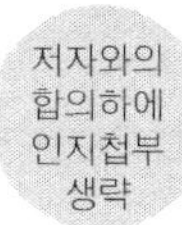

Tourism Hotel English Conversation
(관광호텔영어회화)

2001년 1월 25일 초　　판 1쇄 발행
2012년 9월 10일 초　　판 5쇄 발행
2020년 2월 10일 개정신판 3쇄 발행

지은이 하종명
펴낸이 진욱상
펴낸곳 백산출판사
교　정 편집부
본문디자인 편집부
표지디자인 오정은

등　록 1974년 1월 9일 제406-1974-000001호
주　소 경기도 파주시 회동길 370(백산빌딩 3층)
전　화 02-914-1621(代)
팩　스 031-955-9911
이메일 editbsp@naver.com
홈페이지 www.ibaeksan.kr

ISBN 978-89-6183-744-6
값 15,000원